EDWARD ELGAR
SACRED MUSIC

The Border Lines Series

Series Editor: John Powell Ward

Bruce Chatwin	Nicholas Murray
The Dymock Poets	Sean Street
Edward Elgar Sacred Music	John Allison
Eric Gill & David Jones at Capel-y-Ffin	Jonathan Miles
A.E. Housman	Keith Jebb
Francis Kilvert	David Lockwood
Wilfred Owen	Merryn Williams
Edith Pargeter: Ellis Peters	Margaret Lewis
Dennis Potter	Peter Stead
Philip Wilson Steer	Ysanne Holt
Mary Webb	Gladys Mary Coles
Samuel Sebastian Wesley	Donald Hunt
Raymond Williams	Tony Pinkney

EDWARD ELGAR
SACRED MUSIC

John Allison

Border Lines Series Editor
John Powell Ward

seren

For My Parents

Seren is the book imprint of
Poetry Wales Press Ltd
Wyndham Street, Bridgend, Mid Glamorgan

Text © John Allison, 1994
Editorial and Afterword © John Powell Ward, 1994

A CIP record for this book is available at the
British Library Cataloguing in Publication Data Office

ISBN 1-85411-119-1
1-85411-118-3 pbk

All rights reserved. No part of this publication may be reproduced,
stored in a retrieval system, or transmitted at any time or by any means
electronic, mechanical, photocopying, recording or otherwise, without
the prior permission of the publisher.

*The publisher acknowledges the financial support of the
Arts Council of Wales*

Cover illustration:
Photograph of Elgar by Grindrod, courtesy
of the Elgar Foundation

Printed in Palatino by WBC Book Manufacturers, Bridgend

Contents

7	Prologue: To 1867
18	1. 1867-1889
55	2. 1889-1910
89	3. 1910-1934
116	*Appendix One*
136	*Appendix Two*
137	*Bibliography*
140	*Acknowledgements*
141	*Series Afterword*

Prologue: To 1867

Edward Elgar's music is being seriously regarded again. Even during his lifetime the composer's closeness to his public was treated with condescension in some quarters. The decline of empire decades later, matched by a shift of public opinion, left almost all of Elgar's works, not only the few overtly nationalist ones, unfashionable in intellectual circles. Now, with the passage of time, objective evaluation of Elgar's music is easier, though for the most part this has been limited to his major works; little account has been taken of minor tributaries to the larger stream. One of them was his music for the church. Though sacred music spans his entire creative output, it was of real importance only during Elgar's early, formative years, as the church was one of the few places where the self-taught composer could gain exposure. Stylistic traits of the mature composer are glimpsed in these early pieces, and his upbringing in the Catholic Church shaped his outlook on life. His early experiences of social and religious prejudice played a role in moulding his complex personality.

The aim of this short book is to survey Elgar's sacred music. Many of the works are unpublished and even undocumented, but they are nevertheless worth noting in the context of the composer's life and their place in his output. A proper understanding of Elgar's musical works, from the largest to the most insignificant, can come only through a grasp of the composer's circumstances. For the young Elgar, the church provided a platform and the best available opportunities to practise his craft. His writing for the church during his 'galley' years was prolific, and although many of these compositions have been traced, there is no hope of knowing the full extent of his output. Over the years, many fragments have been scattered widely, and some manuscripts no longer exist. In a 1904 interview, Elgar himself said, 'my juvenile efforts are, I hope, destroyed' (de Cordova: 538). By working through the composer's manuscripts that are preserved in established repositories and by investigating other sources, I have attempted to cover completely the surviving portion of Elgar's church music. To date, no complete list exists, though in due course the Elgar Complete Edition will reach this territory.

In classifying the music, I have defined a piece of sacred music simply as one suitable for performance within the context of a traditional church service. Some pieces not conceived as church music in the strict sense have thus been included. The unaccompanied part-song *The Angelus* has been discussed, but *A Christmas Greeting*, despite the fact that it was written for the choristers of Hereford Cathedral, has been omitted, since the accompaniment is scored for two violins and piano, and the text can hardly be described as sacred. Although it is often classified as a part-song, *Good Morrow* has been included not only because of its text but also because the music was adapted from one of Elgar's early hymn tunes dealt with elsewhere in the book. Late in life, Elgar orchestrated accompaniments to four anthems by other composers (see p. 107), but as they are not original works they are not included. Neither are those movements of Elgar's oratorios which have been published, out of context, as anthems.

Where possible, I have tried to demonstrate a link between Elgar's church works and his more significant compositions. As his sketches show, he often worked simultaneously on several different projects, and many evolved slowly; thus a study of his creative development must take account of all his music. I have drawn on Elgar's writings (mostly published) and other relevant material to give biographical background to the music. These sources have been combined in an attempt to give a full picture of Elgar's music for the church.

Central to the story of Elgar and St George's Catholic Church, Worcester, is the Leicester family. Hubert Leicester (1855-1939) was a contemporary of Elgar's, and a constant companion; he grew up above his father's printing shop at No. 6 High Street, Worcester, and thus close to the Elgars at No. 10. The Leicesters were also Catholic, and about the time that Elgar became organist at St

PROLOGUE: TO 1867

George's, Hubert became choirmaster, a post he kept for the rest of his life. He was an accountant by profession, and became Worcester's first Catholic mayor. Many of his recollections were noted down by his son Philip (1887-1961): these manuscripts, together with Elgar's letters to Leicester, were dispersed at an auction some years ago, but a typewritten transcript of the collection is housed at the Hereford and Worcester County Record Office in the former St Helen's Church, Worcester (where, as a teenager, Elgar used to ring the bells). Throughout this book, quotations concerning the Leicesters are from this source, unless otherwise noted.

Like that of most composers, Elgar's personality embraced many paradoxes. To many observers, Elgar and his music are perceived as 'typically English'. His music may embody the Worcestershire countryside and (outwardly) capture the self-confident essence of Victorian and Edwardian England, but its roots lie in the continental, essentially German, school of composition. Hardly ever did he dabble in the modalism of the English pastoralists who followed him, and he took little interest in either the folksong revival or the Tudor church music that was being rediscovered when he was at the height of his powers. And though England remained fundamental to his musical and social life, the public image of Elgar as an English country gentleman was just one side of an enigmatic individual. From a re-examination of his music and through access to his correspondence now published, we know that beneath the top-hatted Sir Edward, mixing with high society, was a composer who found his inspiration at the deepest levels. But it would be a mistake to deny the 'public' image of Elgar, for although his emotional make-up now seems clear to us, during his life it was changing from day to day.

Perhaps the biggest contradiction came in his religious outlook. Many commentators have noted how the Roman Catholic composer, lionized by Protestant Britain, died apparently a sceptical non-believer, but few have recognized just how atypical his religion made him. Whatever Elgar's final religious feelings were, there is little reason to doubt his faith in his earlier years, especially since the beliefs he clung to were not those of the Establishment. Elgar was the first English composer of the Catholic faith to achieve wide recognition in three centuries, and in *The Dream of Gerontius* he gave expression to Catholicism in a way that no English composer had done before, certainly not since William Byrd three hundred years earlier. A certain spirituality pervades all Elgar's great works, whether religious or not, setting him apart from his contemporaries.

* * *

It was his mother who was responsible for the young Edward's religious upbringing, and her Catholicism made a deep impression on him. Recalling in later life his mother's influence, he said that 'the things she told me I have tried to carry out in my music' (Moore 1984b: 8). Ann Greening, born into a humble family on a farm in the Forest of Dean in 1822, did not convert to Roman Catholicism until 1852, four years after her marriage to William Henry Elgar. Her conversion came about as a result of her husband's work as organist of St George's Catholic Church in Worcester. The composer's daughter recalled: 'Ann Elgar did not like W.H.E. walking alone to Worcester & came to church every Sunday, & eventually went...for instruction & became a Catholic' (Moore 1984a: 5). William Elgar had taken the job in 1846 solely for financial reasons and would have nothing to do with his family's religious arrangements. Edward Elgar's boyhood friend Hubert Leicester recalled the composer's father as 'a regular terror as regards the Catholicity of his family — used to threaten to shoot his daughters if caught going to confession'. In the very year of his wife's conversion he wrote home to his family of 'the absurd superstition and playhouse mummery of the Papist; the cold and formal ceremonies of the Church of England; or the bigotry and rank hypocrisy of the Wesleyan' (Moore 1984a: 6).

William Henry Elgar was born in Dover in 1821. At the age of nineteen he settled in Worcester, after a spell as apprentice to the musical firm of Coventry and Hollier in Dean Street, Soho. Soon he set up a music shop in the Worcester High Street, and much of Edward Elgar's early life revolved around it. Edward was born on 2 June 1857 in a small cottage at Broadheath, two miles from Worcester and within sight of the Malvern Hills. Though the burgeoning family (Edward was the fourth of seven children, of whom five survived) and the demands of William Elgar's business dictated a move back into the city when Edward was two years old, the experiences and surroundings of Broadheath were to

PROLOGUE: TO 1867

shape his whole life. The earliest dated music he wrote was later inscribed 'Humoreske/a tune from Broadheath/1867' (BL Add MS 63154, f. 57v), and when in 1931 he was ennobled, he chose to become the first Baronet of Broadheath.

Edward had been the only one of the children to be born outside the city, but a love of the countryside was nurtured in all the family. The composer's sister Lucy recalled: 'We were always taught to adore Him in the smallest flower that grew, as every flower loves its life. And we were told never to *dare* destroy what we could not give — that was, the life — ever again. There is a humanity in every flower and blade of grass... We were encouraged to go out in all weather during the whole of the year. Although we honestly loved the winter we welcomed the beautiful time of spring: the singing birds had come, hedge and heath, fields and forests were offering their gifts of flowers as a pledge that winter was over' (Moore 1984a: 6-7).

Edward Elgar's earliest musical experiences reflected his father's work as a local musician in Worcester. Using as an analogy the river that runs through Worcester, Elgar recalled for Percy Scholes in 1916 that 'A stream of music flowed through our house and the shop, and I was all the time bathing in it' (Scholes: 343). The thriving Border city supported a number of musical clubs and societies in which William Elgar was active both professionally and socially, but the outstanding feature of the city's musical life was the Three Choirs Festival. Founded probably in 1715 (the exact date is undocumented), the Festival still rotates triennially between Worcester, Hereford, and Gloucester. During Elgar's youth it was perhaps the most important musical event outside London, and it was to dominate the composer's life. As a young boy he attended rehearsals and later became a fully fledged member of the festival orchestra. Years later his music became one of its central features, as it still is today. For the young boy the festival opened exciting new opportunities: it was at the 1866 festival, at a rehearsal for Beethoven's Mass in C (given under the bowdlerised title 'Service in C'), that the nine-year-old first heard an orchestra. William Elgar's services were always in demand during festival time, as a violinist in the orchestra, as a piano tuner, and as a supplier of orchestral parts. He also exerted some artistic influence: it was at his instigation that Cherubini's Mass in D minor and

Hummel's Mass in E-flat were first heard at the Three Choirs Festival (Edwards: 641).

Through his father, Edward made the acquaintance of many musicians, including the organist of Worcester Cathedral, William Done. Though Done was a conservative who is said to have regarded Schumann as a 'modern', Elgar was exposed to a wide range of music in the Cathedral. It was the centre of Worcester's musical life: Done conducted both the Worcestershire Philharmonic Society and the Worcester meetings of the Three Choirs Festival. Elgar frequently acknowledged that his first music was learned by listening in the Cathedral and from books belonging to its ancient music library:

> I drew my first ideas of music from the Cathedral, from books borrowed from the music library, when I was eight, nine or ten. They were barbarously printed in eight different clefs, all of which I learnt before I was 12... I was allowed by Mr Done to borrow them, and they were administered to me by friends who were lay clerks. (Quoted in Moore 1984a: 28)

But the boy's most valuable musical experiences were at his own church, St George's, Sansone Street. The experience of hearing his own pieces performed was vital: at St George's he was able to put his own modest compositions alongside the church music of the day. Music commonly performed in English Catholic churches included works by Haydn, Mozart, Hummel, Cherubini, Spohr, Gounod, Droboisch, Diabelli, Eberlin, and Vincent Novello. Choral music once belonging to William Elgar, now at the Birthplace Museum, includes works by Meyer Lutz, of Southwark Roman Catholic Cathedral. The influence of these composers is evident in Elgar's early work; indeed, there is more of the Catholic idiom in his youthful church music than an affinity with the English church music tradition to which he had been exposed at Worcester Cathedral.

In the 1860s and 1870s, music in England's Catholic churches reflected trends in continental Europe: an English tradition had still to be re-established. With a few notable exceptions, composition in late eighteenth century and early nineteenth century Eng-

PROLOGUE: TO 1867

land had been at a low ebb (native composers were overshadowed by Handel's legacy, by Mendelssohn and other foreign musicians who came to capitalize on the English enthusiasm for music), but the situation in Roman Catholic churches was especially bad, because of discrimination against Catholics. After the Reformation, Mass had been said only in secrecy: its celebration was prohibited, with penalties as for high treason, and even the laity were legislated against. Though the laws were not always enforced, they remained a latent threat. Worse was the prejudice from some quarters of the Protestant public, illustrated in riots which swept London for some days in 1780 (resulting in the death of several hundred people, mainly rioters fired on by troops attempting to control the mob), a reaction against measures of Catholic relief which had passed through Parliament (with only negligible dissent) two years earlier. Though restrictions were gradually lifted, Roman Catholic services continued to be held largely away from the public eye until the Catholic Emancipation Act of 1829.

There had been exceptions; for example, the services held on 'foreign soil' in the chapels of embassies. (The four embassy chapels in London where music flourished were the Spanish, Sardinian, Bavarian and Portuguese.) There, music played an important part in worship. Singers from the Italian opera companies in London, mostly Catholic, gave their services, and fine musicians — notably Vincent Novello (1781-1861), the elder Samuel Webbe (1740-1816), and Samuel Wesley (1766-1837, son of the founder of Methodism, John Wesley, and father of the composer Samuel Sebastian Wesley) — rose to prominence. Novello issued his *Sacred Music as Performed at the Royal Portuguese Chapel* in 1811, thus laying the foundation for the publishing firm Novello and Co., which dominated musical life in nineteenth-century England. He was responsible for introducing the masses of Haydn and Mozart to England and issuing them in vocal score. It was probably his edition of Mozart's Requiem that was used at Carl Maria von Weber's funeral, held at the Catholic Chapel of St Mary, Moorfields, in 1826. The Novello catalogue expanded to provide extensive repertory for churches in England, and St George's Catholic Church in Worcester was one of the many to benefit.

St George's, a Jesuit foundation, was built in 1830, just one year after the Catholic Emancipation Act. Not much is known of the church's musical life until the advent of the Elgars, but, as the family friend Hubert Leicester recalled for the composer's daughter Carice Elgar Blake after her father's death, the Worcester Catholics were in need of an organist when William Elgar was persuaded to take the post in 1846: 'At St George's Church there was a wildly eccentric organist who'd made a fortune in America — could not keep time — had to be superseded on this account' (Moore 1984a: 4). (The reference was probably to an organist named Baldwyn, who preceded Elgar's father.) William Elgar's interest in the church was purely professional. The post was worth forty pounds a year, and he stayed there for thirty-seven years. Years later, his routine was outlined by Elgar and noted down by Philip Leicester: 'Old E. always handed round the snuff box before commencing the Mass, "damned" the blower, and began. Went out at Sermon for a drink at Hop Market'.

The musical life of St George's under the Elgars showed no lack of enterprise, since on ceremonial occasions orchestral accompaniments were common. Standards of musical performance were apparently very respectable. According to the pamphlet 'Notes on Catholic Worcester', written by Hubert Leicester and published in 1928 in anticipation of the centenary of Catholic emancipation, during the first half-century of the church's existence the 'choir supplied the citizens with opportunities for hearing high-class sacred music, rendered in an artistic manner'. In a letter to Leicester written in 1928, Elgar commented that 'touring English opera companies, the personnel of which were mainly Catholic, gave their help, vocal and instrumental, at the Sunday services. Many of the operatic artists were friends of my father'. Elgar recalled that one singer known to have made appearances in the choir loft on several occasions was the Victorian tenor Sims Reeves. The exact composition of the St George's choir is unknown, but given its placing up in the west gallery with the organ, it is likely to have been modest.

The practice of the choir was to sing from separate parts. Some of these part-books, written in various hands, are preserved in the Jesuit Archives at the Farm Street Church, London. There is a copy by William Elgar of the elder Samuel Webbe's Magnificat in A dated April 1848 (Jesuit Archives MS 52/2/2/1); Webbe's music

PROLOGUE: TO 1867

was most influential in shaping English Catholic music of the nineteenth century, and its simple practicality and melodic freshness endeared it to choirmasters and congregations alike. Also preserved are parts headed *Mazzinghi's Mass* (Jesuit Archives MS 52/2/2/1). Joseph Mazzinghi (1765-1844) was an English composer of Corsican origin, and since his reputation rested chiefly on opera, ballet, and chamber music, it is possible that this Mass is an arrangement of a popular stage work. It was an accepted practice during Elgar's youth to make arrangements of sacred music from the secular works of fashionable composers, though more often than not such arrangements were highly inappropriate, the original pieces being chosen for their popularity rather than their suitability. Surviving parts reveal that at St George's the choir also sang arrangements of music attributed to Handel, Mozart, and Mendelssohn.

The archives further confirm what Elgar's early music suggests, a familiarity with the Masses of Classical composers. An alto part-book (Jesuit Archives MS 52/2/1) contains parts for four works, 'Haydn's No. 1 in B-flat' (*Heiligmesse*), 'Haydn's No. 4 in B-flat' (*Schöpfungmesse*), 'Mozart's No. 7 in B-flat' (this work is now known not to be by Mozart: it appears in the Köchel catalogue as KA 233/C1.06 and is thought to be the work of Süssmayer), and 'Mozart's No. 14 in C' (*Missa solemnis*, K 337). Among several others probably performed there, it is known that the choir had Hummel's Mass in B flat in its repertory.

Elgar later recalled that 'from the time I was about seven or eight I used to go and sit by my father and watch him play. After a time I began to try to play myself. At first the only thing I succeeded in producing was noise, but gradually, out of chaos, harmony began to evolve itself' (de Cordova: 538). Eventually he began to assist his father by playing the organ, an instrument that appealed greatly to the young boy. He had begun with the piano, taking lessons from a Miss Sarah Ricketts, who was a member of the St George's choir, but preferred the organ because of its many possibilities; its elaborate ensemble was the closest he could get to the orchestra during those years. Elgar's first biographer recorded that 'he plodded through the "Organ Schools" of Rink and Best without assistance' (Buckley: 8). In his youth it was the organ he used as a means of exploring music, and he persuaded his friend Hubert

Leicester to pump the St George's organ for him. So long as he began with Leicester's favourite composer, Mozart, he could explore whatever he wished. More often than not that included some Wagner.

At St George's, Edward and his family came into contact with Father William Waterworth SJ, priest to the Worcester Catholics from 1858 to 1878, the years of Elgar's boyhood and adolescence. He was a remarkable man, as a Society of Jesus publication recounted in 1883:

> On account of his learning and his kindness and zeal, he was much esteemed by Catholics and Protestants. The Catholics loved him and were proud of him...Dean Peel [of Worcester Cathedral] and many of the Protestant Rectors and Canons were his personal friends. (Quoted in Moore 1984a: 15)

Such qualities were invaluable in a Protestant community where Catholics were treated with suspicion — especially those, like the Elgars, who had converted and therefore could not excuse their religion on the grounds of birth. Catholic emancipation in 1829 had not changed the hearts of many people, and anti-Catholic protests increased after the mass immigration of Irish labourers began during the 1840s. If the working classes feared competition for jobs, many other Protestants were frightened of the allegiance to an authority other than the British sovereign as Defender of the Faith that Catholicism implied. They were distrustful, too, of priests and nuns, and disagreed with Catholic practices, especially veneration of the Virgin Mary, the doctrine of transubstantiation, the petition of saints, and the belief in popular miracles. During his youth, Elgar must have been painfully aware of the religious prejudice around him. In June 1867, the month of his tenth birthday, only twenty miles away in Birmingham, an anti-Catholic meeting degenerated into rioting that had to be broken up by police with sabres. Even as late as the turn of the century, children entering St George's Church were apparently teased by local boys, with such taunts as 'Catholic, Catholic, quack! quack! quack! Go to the Devil and never come back!' (Moore 1984a: 15).

The young Edward's education was in the hands of the Catho-

PROLOGUE: TO 1867

lics. Until around 1860, the only established Catholic class in Worcester was the Poor School at St George's, but before long a local Catholic, Miss Caroline Walsh, started a 'Middle Class School for Girls' in Britannia Square. The old lady's energy was seemingly boundless:

> She used, we are told, to rise very early on Sunday morning for a round among the poor Catholics of the town. Thus she obliged the sluggards to leave their beds and prevented them from missing Mass. Both parents and children held Miss Walsh in veneration. Her lessons were a source of enjoyment to the little scholars, whose hearts she filled with the love of God. The Jesuit priest who had charge of the Mission in Worcester said that the Catholic congregation in that town were largely kept together by the efforts of this Daughter of the Heart of Mary. (Quoted in Moore 1984a: 16)

With no local equivalent of Miss Walsh's school for boys, the young Edward Elgar was obliged to join his sisters at the school in September 1863. Before long William Elgar began to resent his son's Catholic upbringing. One story dating from about his time tells of how Elgar was sitting in his father's shop trying to draw a musical staff; when he finally produced what resembled a Gregorian staff (with only four lines) his father was outraged and jumped to the conclusion that the Catholics were influencing him. Soon William Elgar recognized his son's musical talent, but he would admit it only grudgingly. For the rest of his life, paternal feelings of pride were tinged with jealousy.

1. 1867-1889

William Elgar's duties as a church organist included writing music for the services, but he was a reluctant composer. (An undated *Tantum Ergo* of his survives in the old part-books of the St George's choir, now preserved in the Jesuit Archives MS 52/2/1; a bass part also exists at BL Add MS 49973A: f.13.) Soon he found his son's growing musical talents indispensable. Edward was happy to produce music to suit the varied liturgical requirements, and a considerable amount of his early music was written for St George's. Some of it was used on a regular basis for years afterwards.

The earliest of these compositions seems to have been written when Elgar was about eleven or twelve. In 1868 he left his second school, at Spetchley Park, and moved to Francis Reeve's Academy, at Littleton House across the river at Lower Wick, joining his friend Hubert Leicester there. Elgar's first dated composition, the *Humoreske* from Broadheath, had been written in the summer of 1867. It was incorporated into a musical play by the Elgar children a few years later, themes from which he reworked in the year of his fiftieth birthday as *The Wand of Youth*. The young composer was already responding to the impulses which his mother had nurtured, and so the spiritual side of his upbringing found expression in his early musical efforts too: a simple *Kyrie Eleison* (Appendix One: 1.1). The manuscript is undated, but the juvenile script suggests a date earlier than either his first song *The Language of Flowers* (1872) or an unfinished *Fugue in G minor* (1870): one may guess the year of composition at about 1868 or 1869. Elgar kept the manuscript for most of his life, but gave it to Ivor Atkins, the organist of Worcester Cathedral, in 1929. The short 20-bar setting, in A major, is straightforward and neatly constructed.

At about the time of this first church work, Elgar's parish priest gave him an old French engraving (preserved at the Elgar Birthplace) depicting the Death of St Joseph. The text on the reverse ended with 'Jesus, Mary, Joseph, Pray for me in my own agony', words which Newman had incorporated into his poem *The Dream of Gerontius* a few years earlier. Three decades later Elgar set those words, but for now there were other musical discoveries to be made. The big event of 1869 for Elgar was the Three Choirs Festival in Worcester, and he revelled in the experience of hearing Handel's *Messiah*. The impression that the orchestra left on him made him resolve to learn the violin, and before long he had taught himself enough to join the Worcester Glee Club.

When Elgar left school at the age of fifteen he had, like most boys in his position, to fend for himself. He had hoped to study music, but as there was no money for musical education he went to work in the office of a local solicitor, William Allen, a family friend connected through the church (the firm was situated in Sansone Place, opposite St George's). Within a week of this he played for his first complete service at St George's. His sister Lucy noted in her diary on 14 July 1872: 'Ted played the organ at church for Mass for the first time' (Kennedy: 22).

Probably in 1872, he turned the second movement (*Allegro*) of Mozart's Sonata for Violin and Piano in F, K 547, into a *Gloria* for SATB, soloists, and organ (Appendix One: 1.2). The manuscript of the full score reveals the way in which Elgar adhered strictly to the structure of the piece, pasting vocal parts over the violin line in the printed edition (thin strips of paper to avoid re-writing the accompaniment). This left little room for Elgar's imagination, though he omitted eight bars (122-129) of Mozart's original and inserted his own repeat signs around bars 13-15 (so that the solo soprano's phrase 'Et in terra pax hominibus' could be echoed by the bass soloist singing 'bonae voluntatis'). The piano part of the original made an organ accompaniment virtually as it stood, even though it is unidiomatic in places. Most of the choral writing is original.

Appropriately enough, this arrangement reflects the influence of the Viennese Mass, not least in its use of a quartet of vocal soloists. Elgar's arrangement is much like the Gloria movements in some of the shorter Haydn and Mozart settings in that it is set to an *Allegro* tempo throughout; and the young composer's skilful adaptation of Mozart's score suggests the conventional tripartite Gloria. Elgar introduces the words 'Quonian tu solus sanctuus' at the recapitulation (bar 116); the words with which the final section of a Gloria in tripartite form normally begins.

September 1872 saw Worcester's turn for the Three Choirs Festival come round again, and Elgar was granted permission from his office to attend a *Messiah* rehearsal. But there were tensions developing in the office, where the petty jealousy of a clerk a few years Elgar's senior made the young musician's life unpleasant. Besides, he found the legal work uncongenial; the environment in the Elgar Brothers music shop, where he went to serve in June 1873 as an assistant, was much more to his taste. The shop gave the young Elgar a chance to study textbooks and scores of important works. As he recalled, he was 'self-taught in the matter of harmony, counterpoint, form, and in short, the whole "mystery" of music' (de Cordova: 539). He also had unlimited access to a variety of musical instruments, including the violin, cello, bassoon and piano, which he mastered with varying degrees of success. Elgar was fortunate in coming from a musical family: many other English composers of the period had to endure parental discouragement.

Among Elgar's early musical discoveries, the Beethoven symphonies excited him most. His first biographer, Robert Buckley, recorded the composer's reminiscences of how Beethoven's First Symphony

> convinced him that counterpoint was not the last word of musical art; that Tallis and Byrd and Orlando Gibbons and the rest of the classic church composers had not exhausted the possibilities: that, despite the dicta of the critics and university professors, the 'solid diatonic style' did not represent the the Ultima Thule of composition; and, finally, that Mozart and Beethoven, having attained the highest plane of emotional expressiveness, were the best models for study. (Buckley: 12-13)

His next work, a *Credo* based on themes from Beethoven symphonies (Appendix One: 1.3), reflected that conviction. Whereas in the Mozart *Gloria* arrangement the original had dictated the form, here at least the structure could be his own. Elgar was sixteen years old when he wrote the setting, just one month after leaving the solicitor's office, and the material he used perhaps indicated that he had already found inspiration in the music shop. In the 1904 interview (de Cordova: 540) Elgar recalled that

> In studying scores the first which came into my hands were the Beethoven symphonies. Anyone can have them now, but they were difficult for a boy to get in Worcester thirty years ago. I, however, managed to get two or three, and I remember distinctly the day I was able to buy the Pastoral Symphony. I stuffed my pockets with bread and cheese and went out into the fields to study it. That was what I always did.

Perhaps Elgar also fancied some kind of musical laying-on of hands. For he was no doubt proud of the fact that his father's music teacher in Dover, a Mr Sutton, had himself been a pupil of Beethoven's pupil Ferdinand Ries.

That Elgar was much freer to shape his *Credo* than he had been in his arrangement of the Mozart is evident in the striking modulations he introduced to link the themes, and in some dramatic effects. The influence of the classical Mass is still strong, particularly in the treatment of the 'Et incarnatus' section, where the setting, for a quartet of vocal soloists, is marked *Adagio*. Some of the writing was, on the other hand, unconventional and — for a 16-year-old composer — quite innovative. The text of the *Credo* has frequently presented composers with problems, and most have adopted a 'through-composed' approach. In bars 112-147 of Elgar's early *Credo*, he departs from the normal practice, at 'Crucifixus' opting for an *Allegro* in bold rhythms, where other composers have typically resorted to an *Adagio* setting. Furthermore, he inserted the phrase 'Et incarnatus' between the 'Crucifixus' outbursts. The latter are set boldly for full choir in unison, while the 'Et incarnatus' phrases are sung *piano* by a soprano soloist. (Elgar's treatment of this passage in his 1877 setting of the *Credo* is more conventional.) Although in a sense he was only an arranger rather than a composer, he was already displaying sensitivity to the text and an understanding of musical structure.

For most of this *Credo* the accompaniment is independent of the vocal parts. This is uncommon in Elgar's early church works, most of which are characterized by doubling of voices in the accompaniment, but here Elgar was able to draw on the orchestral lines in Beethoven's music, adapting them freely. Elgar linked Beethoven's themes, taken principally from the first movement of the Fifth Symphony, the second movement of the Seventh, and the third movement of the Ninth, with material of his own. The result reflected the young composer's emotional appreciation of Beethoven, evident also in the works of his maturity, most notably in 'Nimrod' of the 'Enigma' Variations (which suggests the slow movement of the 'Pathetique' Sonata). The *Credo*'s tonal scheme gives notice too of a flatward tendency which was to characterize Elgar's music: though he began in the Seventh Symphony's A minor, he modulated via F major (Beethoven's second subject is in A major), reaching A flat for the 'Et incarnatus', which is based on the slow movement of the Ninth Symphony (a tone lower than Beethoven's B flat major).

The *Credo* survives in two manuscripts. The earlier (Source A) contains some indications of an organ accompaniment, but is incomplete; the other (Source B) appears to have been prepared for performances at St George's, as there are conductor's notes. Generally the two concur, the only significant difference being in the setting of the words 'Et incarnatus'. The later version drew on the opening of the Ninth Symphony, but the earlier manuscript contains different material (probably by Elgar), which is deleted. In this manuscript the young composer showed his modesty (and his small knowledge of German) by signing it 'arranged by Bernard Pappenheim'. Jerrold Northrop Moore even suggests that Elgar, by using the pun 'Pope's home', was already showing a certain detachment from the church, though no more than that of his father. Indeed, William Elgar encouraged his son in other musical directions, introducing him to the operas brought by touring touring companies to Worcester. Elgar recalled hearing the standard works like *Norma*, *La traviata*, *Il trovatore*, and *Don Giovanni* during this period. He heard operatic music in the home, too. His sister Lucy remembered an aria from *La traviata*: 'Mr Allen *always* (yes, every time he came) would sing to Father's accompaniment "Di Provenza il mar"'. Though he never completed an opera, Elgar nurtured a lifelong wish to write one. But for the while the young composer's ambitions had to be satisfied by the church.

Elgar's only other surviving church work from this period is something of a mystery. The manuscript (dated 1874), unsigned but in his hand, is labelled '(Introduction to somebody's Anthem) All Saints' Church Worcester' (Appendix One: 1.4). The seventeen-bar passage, laid out on five staves for strings, is carefully constructed. The melody shows Elgar's early appreciation of Handel but gives no clue to the identity of the anthem. Who requested it and for what occasion it was intended is unclear, especially since all the other church music Elgar wrote until his departure from Worcester in 1889 was composed for St George's. There is no mention in any early correspondence that Elgar had links with the Anglican All Saints' Church, although of course William Elgar's work brought him into contact with other local church musicians.

When it came to the Church of England, it was Worcester Cathedral that claimed most of Elgar's attention:

> I attended as many of the Cathedral services as I could to hear the anthems, and to get to know what they were, so as to become thoroughly acquainted with the English church style. The putting of the fine new organ into the Cathedral at Worcester [1874] was a great event, and brought many organists to play there at various times. I went to hear them all. The services at the Cathedral were over later on Sundays than those at the Catholic Church, and as soon as the voluntary was finished at the church I used to rush over to the Cathedral to hear the concluding voluntary. (de Cordova: 539)

In 1875, after Cathedral restoration and the installation of the new organ, for financial reasons the Dean and Chapter refused permission for a Three Choirs Festival to take place in the Cathedral on the usual full scale. What became known as the 'Mock Festival' consisted instead of a week of choral services (without orchestra) and organ recitals. The latter included one by the great Samuel Sebastian Wesley, from Gloucester Cathedral, whose improvisation and performance of Bach's 'Wedge' Fugue made a life-long impression on Elgar. Though the young musician was denied what would probably have been his first opportunity to play in a festival orchestra, during the ensuing months he played the violin in Cathedral performances of *Messiah*, Spohr's *The Last Judgement*, and Mendelssohn's *Elijah*.

Elgar's next piece of church music, a *Salve Regina* (Appendix One: 1.5), carries hints of the Handel and Mendelssohn oratorios he had recently encountered. He was no longer in need of the assistance of Mozart or Beethoven, but showed enterprise by imitating two of the most popular oratorios of the day, *Messiah* and *Elijah*. The soprano phrase at 'ad te clamamus' bears a striking resemblance to the opening of Handel's 'Behold the Lamb of God', and his setting of this section is similar to Mendelssohn's 'Lord! Bow Thine Ear'. Mendelssohn calls for two soprano soloists over a two-part chorus (sopranos with altos, tenors with basses), and the young Elgar employs two soprano soloists over a two-part choir of tenors and basses.

The *Salve Regina* was written in the summer and autumn of 1876 and shows a great advance in his writing. Elgar must have thought highly of it at the time because in one of the three manuscripts (Source A) he termed it his Opus 1. It was performed at St George's on 6 June 1880, in a special service, attended by Bishop Ullathorne, to mark the opening of a new chancel; other music performed included Hummel's Mass in B flat, works by Haydn and Pergolesi, and Elgar's own *Tantum Ergo* (p. 25). The 141-bar *Salve Regina*, carefully constructed, consists of four distinct sections, each with a different melodic idea.

Characteristic of all his early vocal pieces is the high writing for sopranos, influenced perhaps by string music. Several of his earliest church pieces have wide vocal ranges, sometimes of up to two octaves, and it is interesting that within a few years Elgar's pieces for the same choir made considerably reduced demands. Another feature that emerges in the *Salve Regina* is the parallel movement of parts in thirds (also seen in Elgar's instrumental works from the period, especially in the wind quintets). This *Salve Regina* is also one of the earliest of his works to reveal an 'Elgar trait': there is the poignant descending seventh in the soprano part (bar 61). And it is significant that an harmonic progression which points to Elgar's later style has been marked 'good' by the composer in another of the manuscripts (Source B). Characteristic is his use of the first inversion chord, an effect heightened by what was to become a distinctive Elgarian melodic formula, the juxtaposition of larger intervals (usually fourths, sixths or sevenths) with seconds in descending passages:

Example 1: 'Salve regina', bars 137-8:

(pi) - a ___ O ___ dul - (cis)

Through his *oeuvre*, the composer's 'ripest' moments would often be based on this idea.

Elgar's original Opus 2 was a *Tantum ergo* (Appendix One: 1.6). Written a few months after the *Salve Regina* and bearing a close resemblance to it in its opening, the *Tantum ergo* (two of the three surviving manuscripts, Sources B and C, are dated 27 November 1876), is known to have been performed on the fiftieth anniversary of the founding of St George's, 21 June 1879. It was performed again, along with the *Salve Regina*, on 6 June 1880 at the opening of the new chancel by Bishop Ullathorne. Like the *Salve Regina*, the form is carefully planned, with outer sections in D major and a short middle section in G minor. (In one of the manuscripts, Source A, Elgar marked this with asterisks and noted 'The portion between the stars may be omitted'; this direction has been followed in the third manuscript, Source C, which is not in Elgar's hand.) Perhaps it is not too fanciful to see in this short middle section a glimpse of Elgar's subdominant tendency, which characterized much of the composer's mature music, giving it what Ernest Newman described as its 'sunset quality' (Moore: 1984a: 62). Elgar himself commented on this, when writing to Augustus Jaeger of Novello in 1908: 'I think some of my twists are defensible on *sub*-dominant grounds' (Moore 1987: 710). There are further suggestions of this emerging Elgar trait in other church pieces from the period.

The *Tantum Ergo* is dominated by its opening theme: it returns in a more vigorous guise in the final section, and its contour forms an outline for the more chromatic *Adagio* theme of the middle section. Glimpses of Elgar's mature style are again evident in the way a melody moves up a seventh before falling back. Moreover, the opening of the motet closely resembles a phrase from 'The Little Bells' in the *Wand of Youth* Suite No. 2, which had its origins in music Elgar wrote during these early years.

A *Regina Coeli* (Appendix One: 1.7) survives and was presumably composed during this period. (Though the manuscript is undated, Elgar's handwriting in it is similar to that in the other 1876 manuscripts.) No complete score is known, but the existence of soprano, tenor and bass parts (with indications of an alto line) in the St George's choir part-books suggest that the work was performed. The *Regina Coeli*, an antiphon of the Blessed Virgin Mary, is most commonly used in place of the *Angelus* between Easter and Trinity Sunday, a fact reflected in Elgar's note at the top of the tenor part: 'from Holy Saturday to Trinity Sunday'. The formal structure of the piece is dictated by the distinct sections of the text; an 'Alleluia' is interspersed between each section, suggesting rondo form. The writing is simple but graceful, notably in the *Andante* 'Quia quem meruisti portare', where the soprano soloist sings an almost Mozartian melody that resembles a phrase from the opening of Mozart's *Eine Kleine Nachtmusik*.

Example 2: (a) Elgar: 'Regina coeli', bars 17-18:

(b) Mozart: Serenade in G, K 525, first movement, bars 6-7:

A fragmentary setting of *Psalm 84* (Appendix One: 1.8) also dates from about 1876. The existing music, scored for soprano solo and accompaniment, appears to have been intended as part of something larger, as the marking 'Recit ends' indicates.

Sunday afternoons were set aside for music making with the wind quintet Elgar had formed. Elgar was a competent bassoonist, and with his brother Frank (oboe), the Leicester brothers Hubert (flute) and William (clarinet), and Frank Exton (oboe), he performed music composed during the morning's sermon. 'There was no music to suit our particular requirements so I used to write the music. It was an understood thing that we should have a new piece every week. The sermons in our church used to take at least half an hour, and I spent the time composing the thing for the afternoon' (de Cordova: 540). Elgar called such pieces his 'Shed' music, after the out-house behind the family music shop where the quintet rehearsed. Along with the church music, this was Elgar's main outlet during the period, and the works show the same Classical influences.

In writing for his church, Elgar supplied music as the liturgy required, so it is surprising that no complete settings of the Mass survive. Two early writers suggest that the young composer produced them. Buckley says:

> Motets, masses, all kinds of church music flowed from him in a ceaseless stream. New music for special occasions was always forthcoming from the unofficial assistant organist... (Buckley: 32)

Even earlier, F.G. Edwards, in a 1900 *Musical Times* interview, commented:

> Anyone going into the organ loft of that church may find large manuscript volumes containing many sketches and small compositions...He wrote several Masses and other church music... (Edwards: 645)

And at least one other source suggests that complete Masses existed. When Elgar's *Sursum Corda* (1894) was performed in the Queen's Hall, London, in 1901, the *Malvern Gazette* recorded that 'The piece belongs to a Mass produced some years ago' (Young 1986: 5). (While there is no connection between the *Sursum Corda* and any surviving sketches of church works, it is clear that Elgar derived the main theme of the *Sursum Corda* from an early sketch, the slow movement of an abandoned Violin Sonata of 1887 [BL Add MS 49974D].)

Among fragments from the late 1870s, there are several movements from Mass settings, but none seems to be related to the others, at least not if their tonality is taken as a guide. Soprano and tenor parts for a *Gloria* (Appendix One: 1.9) dated in Elgar's hand 26 June 1877 (and marked by him 'Easy'), are preserved in the old St George's part-books. Cues in these books indicate the existence of a bass part (but no reference to altos) and an organ accompaniment. Set in C major and marked *All[egr]o Spiritoso*, the *Gloria* is 172 bars long and in clear ternary form. It begins boldly with a triadic theme (again, showing Viennese influence), and the middle section ('Gratias agimus tibi') includes an extended soprano solo. The music flows with ease, but there are some large leaps (even ninths) awkward for choristers but more idiomatic for strings — another reflection of the instrumental influences on Elgar's early compositions.

Another part of the Mass from this period (c.1877) is a D minor *Kyrie* for soprano, tenor and bass, marked *Adagio* (Appendix One: 1.10). In ternary form (dictated by the text), the 123-bar piece is thematically concise, with most of the ideas derived from the opening motive. The piece is typical of Elgar's early style, striking dynamic contrasts showing that already early on Elgar was specific in his markings. Two manuscripts survive: one in Elgar's hand (Source A, soprano and tenor parts only) and another, not autograph, which appears to have been made much later. (Although Elgar left St George's in 1889, much of his early music continued to be sung there well past the turn of the century.)

One of the most substantial of Elgar's early church settings is a *Credo* in E minor (Appendix One: 1.11). The only extant manuscript is dated 1877 by the composer (he originally called it his Opus 3), but it is possible that it was written earlier, since Buckley's biography contains a facsimile of a passage from the work. Dated there 1872-3, it is clearly a different manuscript, presumably now lost. The 190-bar piece is divided into four distinct sections, all in E minor. Yet in spite of the tonal scheme, Elgar avoids monotony with some effective modulations and chromatic passages. It is also remarkable in its *pianissimo* opening and conclusion, quite contrary to the conventional declaration of faith, which begins and ends boldly in the major mode. The dignified opening gives way to a graceful, flowing 'Et incarnatus est', followed by a gradually climbing 'Et resurrexit'. The piece also contains an early example of Elgar's *penchant* for descending sequences. An unusually desolate ending is achieved by omitting the third from the final chord, innovative for Victorian church music. Was Elgar recalling the final chords of the first and last movements of Mozart's Requiem? It is also probably not too fanciful to detect also the influence of the Credo from Beethoven's Mass in C, in particular, the chromatic harmonies at 'Et vitam venturi saeculi', and in the rhythms at 'Et unam Sanctam Catholicam'. Like Beethoven — and Haydn in no fewer than four of his 'Six Last Masses' — Elgar took the opportunity of expressing the ideas of 'one Church' by putting the choir in unison:

Example 3 (a): Elgar, Credo, bars 142-146:

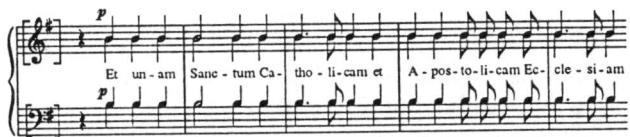

Example 3 (b): Beethoven, 'Mass in C', Credo, bars 257-262:

The phrase at 'Dei unigenitum' foreshadows a phrase in the final movement of *Arthur* (1923), also in E minor:

Example 4 (a): Credo, bars 17-18:

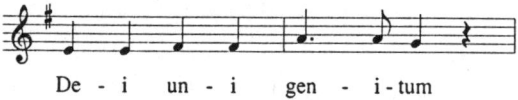

(b): 'Arthur', opening of last scene:

An influence of Catholic, rather than Anglican, church music on Elgar's early sacred works is the way in which opening themes are presented by a solo voice and answered with a harmonised repetition of the same material. A well-known example is the opening of the *Ave Verum* (the *Pie Jesu* of 1887), but an earlier instance occurs in the 'Et incarnatus' section of the *Credo*:

Example 5: Credo, voice parts only, bars 45-56:

Elgar is known to have composed at least six settings of the *O Salutaris Hostia*. The earliest of these is in G major for voice and organ, written c. 1877 (Appendix One: 1.12). The work (in ternary form) is fluent but resembles a light secular piece rather than a setting for the service of Benediction. The writing again reflects the influences of secular music, rather than sacred, in Elgar's early church works. Some passages show his instrumental approach to the voice; others, for instance the closing cadenza, are almost operatic:

Example 6 (a): 'O Salutaris Hostia', bars 27-29:

Example 6 (b): 'O Salutaris Hostia', bars 48-50:

One manuscript (Source A) is undated, but the first page of another copy (this time in A major), presumably lost, is reproduced in Buckley's biography with the comment 'composed when

Elgar was a boy'. In the surviving manuscript there is no indication of the voice-type Elgar had in mind, but the facsimile of the A major version is clearly marked 'Contralto'. This may be of some significance, since in later life the voice-type appealed greatly to Elgar: many of his finest vocal settings are for contralto, including his only song-cycle with orchestra, *Sea Pictures* (1897-9), and *The Music Makers* (1902-12), scored for contralto soloist, chorus and orchestra.

Though Elgar's dream of going to Leipzig to study was never to be fulfilled, in 1877 he did scrape together enough money for a twelve-day visit to London to hear concerts and to have five lessons with Adolf Pollitzer, the leader of the Philharmonic Society Orchestra and of the Opera Orchestra, Covent Garden. (Pollitzer's links with Mendelssohn — he had performed the composer's Violin Concerto in his presence — must have been an attraction for Elgar, since the German composer was one of the youthful Elgar's heroes.) More valuable than the lessons, however, was the introduction which Pollitzer gave Elgar to August Manns, whose regular Crystal Palace concerts were a feature of London's musical life. Elgar became a regular visitor to London, armed with a rehearsal pass courtesy of Manns:

> I rose at six, walked a mile to the railway station, the train left at seven; arrived at Paddington about eleven, underground to Victoria, on to the Palace arriving in time for the last three-quarters of an hour of rehearsal; if fortune smiled, this...included the work desired to be heard; but fortune rarely smiled and more often than not the principal item was over. Lunch. Concert at three. At five a rush to Victoria; then to Paddington, on to Worcester arriving at 10.30. A strenuous day indeed; but the new work had been heard...
> (Moore 1984a: 79)

Back home Elgar struggled on. He still cherished an ambition to become a solo violinist, and that repertory is reflected in an *O Salutaris Hostia* written about this time (Appendix One: 1.13), which survives only in a fragmentary sixteen-bar soprano part (there are indications for an organ introduction). Elgar noted 'Paganini' at the top of the page, indicating that the melody is an adaptation of Paganini's Caprice in G minor for solo violin. Elgar's arrangement of the music is straightforward and follows the original closely, retaining the *Adagio* tempo indication but transposing the music into E minor. He set the text strophically, as in most other of his settings of the text, inserting the words of the second verse under those of the first.

Example 7 (a): Paganini: Caprice Op. 1 No. 6, bars 1-4:

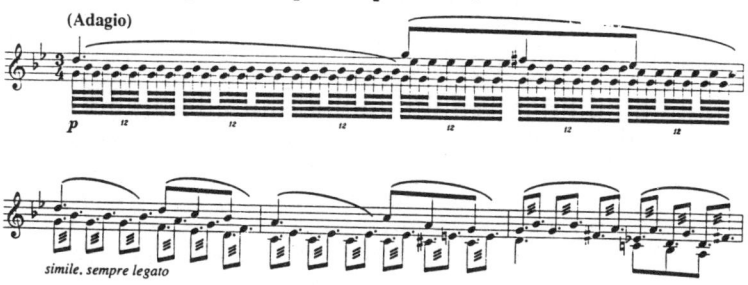

Example 7 (b): Elgar, 'O Salutaris Hostia', bars 1-4:

Several parts of the Mass survive in incomplete sketches Elgar made during the late 1870s. One consists simply of two chords marked 'Sanctus' (Appendix One: 1.16), the only 'setting' of this text known to exist, in a sketch-book dated 13 August 1878. Most of the sketches in this book were written during that year, including Elgar's symphonic exercise based on Mozart's Symphony No. 40 in G minor, K 550, and an incomplete *Kyrie Eleison* in C minor (Appendix One: 1.15). A fragmentary *Credo* (consisting mainly of the soprano line, with some indication for the bass and organ parts) is found in a sketch-book that the composer signed and dated 'Edward Wm Elgar/May 21:78' (Appendix One: 1.14). It is undistinguished; so is an incomplete *Gloria* (Appendix One: 1.25) sketched in a book begun on 7 April 1879 and probably written during that year.

During this period Elgar made two settings of the *Magnificat*. The first, in G major, undated but contained in a sketch-book begun on

13 August 1878, is notable for its well-proportioned opening (the voices enter imitatively) and a chromatically shifting organ accompaniment (Appendix One: 1.17). The same book has an F major setting (Appendix One: 1.23) that begins boldly in octaves; Elgar evidently returned to the piece some months later as the same material (plus a contrasting passage at the words 'Esurientes implevit bonis') exists in another book begun on 1 October 1878.

In the month of Elgar's twenty-first birthday, June 1878, a notice appeared in the Catholic magazine *The Tablet*:

> To Musical Catholic Noblemen, Gentlemen, Priests, Heads of Colleges, &c., or Professors of Music. — A friend of a young man, possessed of great musical talent, is anxious to obtain partial employment for him as Organist or Teacher of Piano, Organ, or Violin, to young boys, sons of gentlemen, or as Musical Amanuensis to Composers or Professors of Music, being a quick and ready copyist. Could combine Organist and Teacher of Choir, with Musical Tutor to sons of noblemen, &c. Has had several years experience as Organist. The advertiser's object is to obtain musical employment for him, with proportionate time for study. Age 21, of quiet, studious habits, and gentlemanly bearing. Been used to good society. Would have unexceptionable references. Neighbourhood of London preferred; the Continent not objected to. Disengaged in September. Address Alpha beta, TABLET Office. (Moore 1984a: 78)

It drew no response. Instead, in January 1879 Elgar took up one of the more unusual appointments ever held by any composer: Bandmaster of the Attendants Orchestra at the Worcestershire County Lunatic Asylum, Powick. His duties included conducting and composing; each work produced earned him five shillings on top of his thirty-two pounds annual salary.

On St George's Day 1879, Elgar's older sister Pollie married William Grafton, a member of a prominent local Catholic family. There is no record of the musical arrangements for the ceremony at St George's, and if Elgar wrote anything special for that occasion it does not appear to have survived.

Two more substantial church works were written in the spring of 1879. The *Domine Salvum Fac* (Appendix One: 1.24) was composed not long before its first performance on 21 June 1879 at a service to commemorate the fiftieth anniversary of St George's. Like the earlier *Tantum Ergo* and *Salve Regina* (see pp. 24-26), it was performed again on 6 June 1880 when Bishop Ullathorne opened the new chancel. Elgar's loyalty to the Queen is expressed in the words of the anthem, 'Domine salvum fac Reginam nostram Victoriam'. Perhaps he was making a deliberate statement, since one of the Victorians' objections to Catholicism was the double allegiance to Pope and Crown that it implied. Sketches for the *Domine Salvum Fac* show that Elgar scored the accompaniment for strings and wind rather than organ. Even at this early stage the future composer of oratorios was not content to limit himself to choir and organ only. Again, there are shades of Mozart here. Like many of his earlier church works, the *Domine Salvum Fac* shows Classical influences in its melodies:

Example 8 (a): 'Domine Salvum Fac', bars 9-15:

Example 8 (b): 'Domine Salvum Fac', BL Add MS 63149: f. 19v.:

Scales and arpeggios characterise the melodic writing of his early chamber music, too, as this extract from a String Trio dated 20 August 1878 (BL Add MS 63147: f. 3) shows:

Example 9: String Trio, Violin I, bars 1-5:

(Elgar also used this material in one of his Wind Quintets, *Shed 4*.)

The other church work written during this time, *Brother, for thee He died* (Appendix One: 1.26), was apparently never completed. It appears in a sketch-book dated 7 April 1879 and is marked 'Easter', but since Easter fell that year on 13 April, Elgar was probably unable to finish the work and never returned to it. The title gives some clue to the circumstances behind the composition. Two of Elgar's brothers died in childhood: Harry, who was older than Edward, died in May 1864, and Jo, a younger brother, in September 1866. Though death was an ever-present threat to families of this period, these losses left a deep mark on the Elgars. Edward's sister Lucy recalled the first of the deaths as 'a great great sorrow, a very real sorrow — the death of my brother Harry, after an illness of four weeks only. This grief nearly cost my Father his reason, but by my Mother's bravery and fortitude that awful calamity was averted' (Moore 1984a: 27). Edward was left as the oldest son, bearing the burden of his family's aspirations. Of the composition of the anthem, Jerrold Northrop Moore comments that 'At a time when most of the surviving children were beginning to find their ways in the world, it must have been impossible not to think sometimes of Harry, the eldest son and brother — or of Jo, whose musical promise would now have been approaching maturity' (Moore 1984a: 88).

The piece has some striking musical features which set it apart from other of Elgar's early church works, and though it is incomplete, a sense of thematic unity is evident. The opening is notable for its deferred phrase ending: five bar phrases were not common practice in Victorian church music. Rhythms are strong throughout, and the music is characterized by a recurrent 'weeping' motif. The organ accompaniment is reminiscent of another sketch in the same book, for an Organ Concerto, also in D minor, evidence again of how the young composer's thoughts were transferred from one work to another. Elgar's choice of tonality is interesting, especially since he did not use this key widely in other early church works: considering the nature of the music, it may well echo Mozart's use of D minor in the Requiem, a work that Elgar encountered as a violinist when it was performed at the Worcester Festival of 1878. The festival filled up Elgar's diary that September: other works given included *Messiah*, *Elijah*, Mendelssohn's *Hymn of Praise*, Part I of *Creation*, Spohr's *Last Judgement*, Mozart's Symphony No. 40 (K550), and new English works such as Armes's *Hezekiah* and Stainer's *Daughter of Jairus*.

1867-1889

During these years Elgar also produced several hymn tunes, most of which are of little importance. For the words 'Now with the fast departing light' he wrote a simple G major tune (Appendix One: 1.18) which appeared as No. 89 in a collection of hymns compiled by Hubert Leicester for use at St George's in 1878. Alto and tenor parts only survive for a hymn 'By the blood that flowed from Thee' (Appendix One: 1.22), and the number '104' on the tenor part indicates that it too belonged to the collection of hymns. No. 63 is a setting of 'Praise ye the Lord: on ev'ry height' (Appendix One: 1.20) of which versions survive in at least five manuscript sources. Elgar thought well enough of this tune to use it as the basis for a late work, the carol *Good Morrow* (see page 109) of 1929, with, of course, some refinements. Another tune (Appendix One: 1.21) lacks words, but the number '80' in the manuscript suggests that it may have been included in Leicester's 1878 collection, though the unadventurous, static part writing may mean that it had been written some years earlier.

The only significant one of these early hymn tunes is 'Hear Thy children gentle Jesus', dated 21 July 1878 (Appendix One: 1.19). Despite its humble beginnings in the 1878 collection (set originally to a translation by R. Campbell of the hymn 'Verbum supernum'), it became the composer's best-known hymn tune, after Elgar's use of it in his *Nursery Suite* (see below). It was published in two hymn books (*Tozer's Catholic Hymns* and the *Westminster Hymnal*) in 1898, but appeared in print even earlier, in *The Catholic Hymnal* published in Dublin in 1896. The tune appeared in subsequent editions of the *Westminster Hymnal* (1912, 1927 and 1939), and it is in the last of these that the name 'Drakes Broughton' appeared, although it was mis-spelt as 'Drakes Boughton'. (The tune remains in favour, as its publication in the 1983 Methodist *Hymns and Psalms* proves.)

Drakes Broughton, from which Elgar took the name of the tune, is a village near Pershore in Worcestershire. Elgar told one of his early biographers that he intended to haunt a wooded lane nearby:

> And in fancy he likes to think of himself in the years beyond life itself, moving leisurely along those green ways, perchance to surprise an old friend there who had accustomed himself to think of him as being eternally absent. There is one road in particular to which he intends to return,

a secluded stretch of about a quarter of a mile which even at summer's noon is darkened by tall trees, so that its shadow and its silence are one in their depth. It is not far from Drakes Broughton. (Maine, I: 166)

The tune's simplicity and purity was contrary to the prevailing fashion of the day when so many hymn tunes wallowed in chromaticism. Though it is unpretentious, Elgar must have held it in affection, for he used it in the first movement (Aubade) of the *Nursery Suite* in 1931. As in many of his late compositions, Elgar returned to early sketches as part of a conscious harking back to his childhood and youth. He commented in a programme note for the suite:

> The first movement...should call up memories of happy and peaceful awakenings; the music flows in a serene way; a fragment of a hymn tune ('Hear Thy children, gentle Jesus' — written for little children when the composer was a youth) is introduced; the movement proceeds to develop the opening theme, the hymn is repeated more loudly and dies away to a peaceful close: the day has begun. (Moore 1984a: 787)

Over half a century before Elgar used the hymn in the *Nursery Suite* he saw the possibility of arranging it for instruments, setting out the hymn (BL Add MS 63147: f. 6v.) as a theme for a set of variations for wind quintet. This was never completed.

Not much is known about an A flat major hymn tune (Appendix One: 1.28) contained in a sketch book dated 'April 7: 1879'. In its simple diatonic harmonies is it reminiscent of 'Hear Thy children, gentle Jesus', and it appears that Elgar returned to this tune too as part of a project towards the end of his life. In the old book the hymn is labelled 'Richardson' in the composer's mature writing. This is probably a reference to a request in 1931 from the architect Sir Albert Richardson for Elgar to compose a chime for the church at Eaton Socon, Bedfordshire (now Huntingdon), which he was restoring. The church had been destroyed by fire in 1930, and Richardson was in charge of the restoration, which was completed in 1932. He was acquainted with Elgar from Brooks's Club in London and wrote to him on 11 March 1931 requesting the chime.

The composer was initially reluctant to help and wrote 'Answer No' (Houfe: 119) across the top of the letter. Later, after some coercion, he sent a manuscript to Richardson. Once the music was in the hands of the church, events took an unfortunate turn, as Richardson's grandson relates:

> The manuscript was sent straight on to the vicar at Eaton Socon, but unfortunately difficulties were already crowding in on this valiant attempt to introduce distinctive chimes for the rebuilt church. After Elgar's music had arrived, the Council in one of those wild moments that provincials are capable of suddenly decided to make their chimes a matter of open competition and invited several musicians to submit compositions. Sir Sydney H. Nicholson and Mr S.G. Wilkinson [the local organist] of Eaton Socon submitted music and these compositions were considered along with Elgar's. My grandfather was horrified as he saw his generous ideas being mutilated, the difficulty of placating Elgar was also uppermost in his mind. (Houfe: 121)

The manuscript was eventually returned to the composer, but its fate is unknown. (A full account of this debacle appears in Simon Houfe's biography of his grandfather, *Sir Albert Richardson: the Professor*.)

During the morning sermons at St George's, Elgar continued to write music for the wind quintet. His activities as a local musician were constantly increasing. For the Attendants Orchestra at the Powick asylum he composed works with such titles as *Der junge Kokette* and *Paris*, the latter a result of his first trip abroad, to France in 1880, in the company of his future brother-in-law Charles Pipe. Together they heard Saint-Saëns at the organ of La Madeleine, went to the theatre to see a Molière play, and visited the tombs of Rossini and Bizet.

Round about 1880 Elgar produced another *O Salutaris Hostia*, a four-part setting (with organ accompaniment) in E-flat major (Appendix One: 1.30). The only surviving manuscript copy, not in Elgar's hand, is marked '(M. Grafton)' — a reference probably either to his niece May Grafton or his sister Pollie Grafton (whose full names were Susannah Mary) — and appears to have been made at a later date. (There are some discrepancies between it and the published version: it lacks the 'Amen' of the published edition, some of the part-writing is different, and it includes an organ introduction not printed.) Though most of the choral writing is conventional, it reveals Elgar's sensitivity to the text. Lines overlap and are repeated freely, a feature not found in many of his other church pieces, but a technique he went on to develop fully in the large-scale choral works of the 1890s.

In 1889 Alphonse Cary published the *O Salutaris* as No. 21 in a series 'Modern Music for Catholic Choirs', and it appeared in print again in the 1898 edition of 'Tozer's Benediction Manual', along with another setting of the text in F major (Appendix One: 1.35) which Elgar probably composed at about the same time. The latter is probably the piece mentioned in Hubert Leicester's letter to Elgar of 1 October 1899, where he refers to 'the original M.S. of the "O Salutaris": 'Pray accept my hearty thanks for same, it is a link with the past, & reminds me of our old happy times. I hope some day to sing the "O Salutaris" at Benediction'. Of all Elgar's early church settings, the F major *O Salutaris* is perhaps the best proportioned. Although the writing is straightforward, there is a lovely, Elgarian sequence dripping in appogiaturas (bars 9-12), a striking passage which points to the mature Elgar:

Example 10: 'O Salutaris Hostia', bars 9-12:

Percy Young has suggested that the evocative, almost mystical 'Amen' looks forward to the seraphic chorus in *The Dream of Gerontius*:

Example 11: 'O Salutaris', bars 14-19:

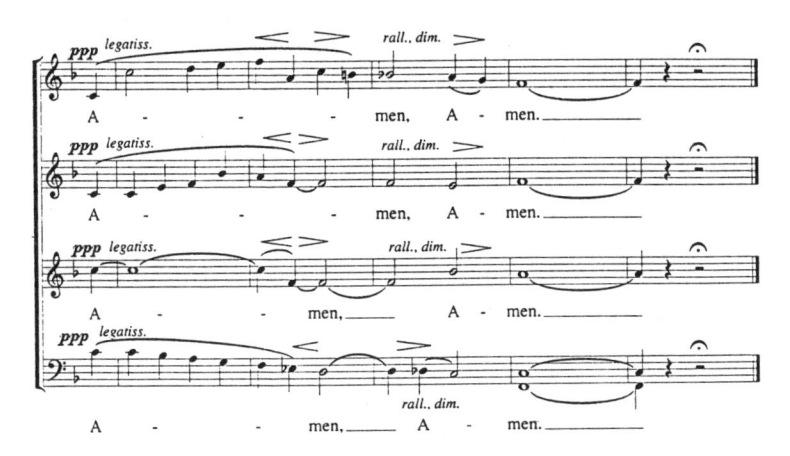

[musical notation]

A similar mystical feeling pervades parts of an *O Salutaris Hostia* for bass solo, chorus ad lib., and organ, signed and dated 'Ap. 17. 1882 Ed. W^m. Elgar' (Appendix One: 1.32). Though a short setting of only seventy-seven bars, it is a landmark in the development of Elgar's style as it already displays several features which were to become recognizable traits of his music. The surviving manuscripts are incomplete, but a wide range of expression is nevertheless evident, and Elgar's treatment of the text is free. Most interesting is the way in which a passage of the organ accompaniment closely resembles the opening of *King Olaf*, which appeared fourteen years later.

Example 12 (a): 'O Salutaris Hostia', sketch for organ accompaniment, bars 41-45:

[musical notation]

Example 12 (b): 'King Olaf' (opening), bars 4-5:

This was indeed an important period in the development of the composer: besides *King Olaf* (1896), parts of *The Black Knight* (1893) have their origins in music written in the late 1870s and early 1880s.

A spare page in one of the manuscripts of this *O Salutaris* contains the barest outline for a *Kyrie Eleison* (Appendix One: 1.33), presumably sketched during the same period. An incomplete *Gloria* (Appendix One: 1.31) written around this time is preserved in a sketch-book begun on 1 September 1881. Much of the writing is clumsy, with some extravagant modulations.

A hymn-like setting of *O Salutaris Hostia*, also in E flat major (Appendix One: 1.29), is undated, but stylistic features suggest that it is unlikely to have been written before 1880. Though simple, it is arguably the most expressive of Elgar's early hymn tunes.

In September 1881 Elgar played in the orchestra for the Three Choirs Festival, once again at Worcester. The orchestration of Alexander Mackenzie's cantata *The Bride* made an impression on him, but a far greater thrill was hearing Berlioz's music the following month in London. A St James's Hall concert Elgar attended included *Nuits d'été* and the overture to *Die Meistersinger von Nürnberg*. Hans Richter was the conductor: five years earlier Richter had conducted the *Ring* at the opening of Wagner's Festspielhaus at Bayreuth, and he was to play a significant role in Elgar premieres in the years to come.

By 1882 Elgar was leading a busy life and had established a considerable local reputation. Some of his small orchestral works were being performed by local ensembles, including the Amateur Instrumental Society in Worcester, of which Elgar became the conductor in 1882. That year they played his *Air de Ballet* at the British Medical Association's jubilee meeting, and Elgar invited one of the younger delegates who was also an accomplished

1867-1889

amateur cellist, Dr Charles Buck, to join the orchestra. The two men struck up a friendship which lasted until Buck's death in 1932: Elgar visited him at his home in Giggleswick, Yorkshire, and corresponded frequently. The letters give insights into his life at this time, which, as he confided to Buck on 31 October 1882, was very full indeed:

> I am 'so busy' really but get no time to myself. This is, of course, all very nice from a commercial point of view, but Oh! my fiddling; I never touch it now save to give lessons or scrape at a Concert. (Young 1956: 4)

His busy schedule may account for the fact that a *Benedictus* dated 7 May 1882, like many of his pieces from this period, appears never to have been completed (Appendix One: 1.34). Even so, the manuscript shows that Elgar had some details fixed in his mind: the bars (53 in all) are ruled out, and, though many have been left blank, others have detailed dynamic markings. The work is scored for voices, strings, and organ, and the graceful writing has features in common with some of Elgar's early string pieces, the key (G major) and time signature (12/8) recalling perhaps the 1878 *Romance* for violin and piano (eventually published as his Op. 1).

At the end of the year Elgar achieved his long-held ambition of visiting Leipzig, not to study, however, but for a short holiday and to attend concerts and opera. His friend Frank Weaver, whose family had a bootmakers' shop in the Worcester High Street, helped him with the arrangements. Frank's sister Helen and her friend were students at the Leipzig Conservatory, and Frank advised Elgar to stay at the same pension as the girls. Elgar arrived in Leipzig on New Year's Eve 1882 and spent his fortnight going to concerts with them. He recalled: 'I got pretty well dosed with Schumann (my ideal!), Brahms, Rubinstein, and Wagner, so had no cause to complain' (Moore 1984a: 97). Among the music he heard was the Prelude to *Parsifal*, which had had its first performance in Bayreuth only a few months previously.

Before long he and Helen Weaver — whose name had already been inscribed at the top of several of his pieces (a Polka marked 'H J W vom Leipzig gewidmet' survives at the Birthplace) — were in love, and Elgar looked forward eagerly to her return to Worcester, as he confided to Buck on 1 July 1883: 'The vacation at Leipzig begins shortly, my "braut" arrives here on Thursday next; remaining 'till the first week in Septr; of course I shall remain in Worcester 'till her departure' (Young 1956: 8). When she returned at the end of the Leipzig term, they became unofficially engaged: their families were anxious that nothing should be announced until their religious differences — the Weavers were Unitarians — could be resolved.

At the end of 1883 Elgar's prospects were good, and for the 26-year-old composer the year was crowned when he gained his first musical exposure outside Worcester and its surroundings. Elgar had been playing for W.C. Stockley's Popular Concerts in Birmingham for some time when the conductor included the young man's *Intermezzo mauresque* in his programme on December 13.

Meanwhile, he continued to assist his father at St George's until church politics intervened just before Christmas that year. He wrote to Buck:

> ...the younger generation at the Catholic Church have taken an objection to him and got him turned out of the Organist's place: this he held for 37 years!! He thinks a great deal of this and I fear 'twill break him up. (Young 1955: 52)

Soon Elgar's letters to Buck were tinged with sadness. Things with Helen were not going smoothly: she had been forced to abandon her studies to tend to her dying mother, and within a few months they broke off their engagement. Elgar wrote to Buck on 20 July 1884: '...my prospects are worse than ever & to crown my miseries my engagement is broken off & I am lonely' (Atkins: 479). The following year Helen Weaver, having contracted tuberculosis, sailed for New Zealand in search of a gentler climate (she died there in 1927) and Elgar, nursing a broken heart at Charles Buck's in Yorkshire, set his touching song *Through the long days and years*: 'Never on earth again shall I before her stand'.

In London in May 1884 he attended the first British performance of Brahms's Third Symphony (conducted by Richter). An even greater excitement was playing in the orchestra at the Worcester Festival that year under Dvořák's baton, an experience that once again fired his own ambitions and opened his eyes to musical life beyond the confines of the English provinces. One month after the festival he resigned his conductorship of the Powick Asylum Band.

At home, the loss of his father's job as organist still threatened family relations. He wrote to Buck on 29 October 1885:

> The old man does not take kindly to the Organ biz: but I hope 'twill be all right before I commence my 'labours'. (Moore 1984a: 113)

Elgar took over as organist of St George's, but diffused the difficult situation by allowing a decent interval of time to elapse before commencing his duties on a regular basis. He approached the job seriously, drawing up a list of regulations together with Hubert Leicester, who worked as choirmaster alongside him, to ensure that things ran smoothly. There is a reference to proofs of the rules in Elgar's letter to Leicester of 20 August 1886, and a note written to him from Patterdale, Ullswater, on 29 August gives a clue to the date of Elgar taking up the post:

> I was very glad to get your letter & to hear that Fr Foxwell had given our production 'Imprimatur'. It ought to have some effect on the Choir generally & I am anxious to see how it is taken by the Members...I shall be with you on Sunday & after that I hope we shall begin the regeneration of the Church Music in good earn.

Rule No. 4 reads:

> The Members to conform in all Musical matters to the instructions of the Organist, whose authority on all questions of Music shall be supreme...(BL Add MS 60357, f. 8)

That apparent severity obscures the way in which Elgar's humour came out in the job, not least in his choice of voluntaries:

> ...he officiated at a baptismal service, and as at that time he was greatly attached to Berlioz's *Symphonie fantastique*, he extemporised the 'March to the Gallows' as the worshippers were leaving the church.

EDWARD ELGAR: SACRED MUSIC

> All left but one man, who lingered, and approaching young Elgar said, 'Excuse me, I am the father of the boy that was baptized, and I should like to know the name of the beautiful tune you were playing'.
> Elgar thought rapidly and cautiously replied, 'Oh! that was a march by a French composer'. (Gaisberg: 246-7)

Early in January 1886 Elgar wrote to Buck: 'I have retired into my shell in the hopes of writing a polka someday — failing that a single chant is probably my fate' (Moore 1984a: 113). Indeed, that year brought a short hymn tune set to the 'Stabat Mater dolorosa' (Appendix One: 1.36). Two manuscripts of the F major tune survive; Source B is signed and dated March 1886.

Elgar's feelings of frustration with the job were already emerging. In the letter written to Buck just after the New Year, he had added: 'I am a full fledged organist now & HATE it. I expect another three months will end it; the choir is awful & no good to be done with them' (Moore 1989: 15). But he endured, and began to work closely with the St George's priest, Father Knight. Together they compiled a book of Litanies (Appendix One: 1.37) for the church's use. Four were issued by Cary in 1888 — the first publication of any of Elgar's church music — as *Four Litanies of the Blessed Virgin Mary*, and dedicated to Father Knight. The four litanies (two in D major and two in E major) appeared along with two of Elgar's chants (in D major and E major); the litanies (but not the chants — others were substituted) were reissued in another Cary publication, Tozer's *Complete Benediction Manual* in 1898 (and in subsequent editions). Elgar's melodies, simple as they are, have direction, a feature almost completely lacking in the majority of the other chants published alongside in the Benediction Manual. Elgar mentioned his chants to the Leicesters in 1919:

> Conversation at dinner was general, till E. got on music. Between courses he suddenly went to the piano to illustrate how Tozer in publishing his Benediction services had amended the harmonies to suit his (Tozer's) taste. He played Tozer's version of the Litany, & then his own harmonies as originally written, the two things being absolutely different. Father was furious, E. only laughed.

Perhaps the mature composer was making excuses for his juvenile efforts: the manuscripts reveal no significant differences with the published version.

Different manuscripts survive, the most important being a book of litany chants (numbered up to twenty-seven, but some are missing), mostly in Elgar's hand, and signed and dated 1887 (Source A). Judging from its well-worn appearance and traces of candle wax, it appears to be the copy which Elgar used at the organ. There is also a copy (Source C), in Hubert Leicester's hand, of fourteen of the chants in the original. All the chants here are dated September 1886, probably the date of the compilation of the original collection. We know that Elgar was assembling them during that year from a letter dated 15 July 1886 to Leicester: '6 cop. ea[ch] of four chants' (BL Add MS 60357: f. 1). All of the chants here are attributed to 'F & E Elgar', a suggestion that Elgar's brother Frank may have had a hand in the composition or arrangement. Elgar made occasional attempts to encourage his brother's creative talents, but the extent of their collaboration is unclear, and the other manuscripts attribute the chants to Edward Elgar only. The latest known litany manuscript (Source B) is in the composer's hand, made in 1931 when he presented a copy of a chant and litany to Ivor Atkins. Significantly, Elgar dated the music as 1876, the earliest date given anywhere for the litanies, and, if Elgar's memory was serving him correctly, evidence that the litanies were composed over a number of years. He added one in 1890, written for St George's a year after leaving the church, and Leicester acknowledged it in a letter of 22 June: 'It was good of you to do the Litany for us, & I am now going to make copies of it for the choir...There certainly is your "private mark" stamped upon it'.

Those copied into the book by Elgar came from disparate sources, perhaps another indication that the collection evolved slowly. Not all of the settings are by Elgar himself. Two are acknowledged as being taken from litany chants in *Hymns Ancient and Modern*, and one other is an arrangement of the well-known hymn-tune 'Innocents'. A wide range of sources seems to have been drawn on (underneath one Elgar noted 'N.B. Maister Edwarde Elgar dide notte harmonise ye above, God wot!'); another bears Elgar's comment that it was based on an Air by Ricci, from an opera 'introduced here by F. Walmisley'.

EDWARD ELGAR: SACRED MUSIC

Elgar was approaching thirty when he wrote what is today probably his best known piece of church music, the *Ave Verum* (Appendix One: 1.38). It was published in 1902 when the composer was at the height of his powers, but dates back to the Worcester days. The music started life as a *Pie Jesu*, written in memory of his boyhood employer, the Worcester solicitor William Allen. There are three surviving manuscripts; Source A is inscribed 'In Memoriam — W.A. — Obit. Jan 27:1887' and signed and dated 'Edward Elgar Jan. 28:87', thus indicating that it was written on the day after Allen's death.

The *Ave Verum* has a simple tune, with characteristic descending steps. At its climax, Elgar uses the same 'fingerprint' first inversion chord and melodic formula seen earlier in the *Salve Regina* (p. 24). But he seems to have been worried about other less 'Elgarian' passages: at the bottom of one of the old *Pie Jesu* manuscripts (Source B), he noted 'Very like "Love Divine" in Daughter of Jairus, Stainer'. Indeed, it is. Stainer's cantata received its premiere at the Worcester Festival of 1878, with Elgar among the second violins on that occasion. In its original guise, the music is even simpler than in its published form, being scored for sopranos and organ only. In 1902 he expanded the score, repeating each half and introducing full choir; to accommodate the new text, he added the characteristic Elgarian coda of six bars, which some commentators have mistaken for an early glimpse of his mature style.

Elgar's affection in later life for his youthful pieces has often been noted, but it was probably in response to a request from Jaeger on behalf of Novello that he took out the score of the *Pie Jesu* and re-set it as the *Ave Verum*. Dispatching it to the publishers on 20 January 1902, he added a note that the music 'is too sugary I think but it is nice & harmless & quite easy'. The *Ave Verum* was soon published with English words under the title *Jesu, Word of God Incarnate*. Towards the end of his life, in 1930, Elgar produced another arrangement of the piece, after receiving a suggestion from an Oxfordshire schoolmistress for an adaptation for female voices. Elgar rejected her advice but took up the idea himself and produced a version for which he persuaded Novello to pay seven guineas instead of the proffered five (Moore 1987: 868).

On 25 March 1902, Elgar wrote to Novello about the *Ave Verum* and hinted at future pieces:

> As this is an early work I would like to let it be unobtrusively known that it is so: may I therefore call it Op.2.No.1. It's not long enough for an Op. all to itself — & amongst the heaps of similar things I wrote when a youth may find something which may do for further numbers. (Moore 1987: 329)

In the event, it was to be some five years before Op. 2 Nos 2 and 3 appeared. They are an *Ave Maria* (Appendix One: 1.39) and an *Ave Maris Stella* (Appendix One: 1.40), both revised versions of early pieces probably also written in the late 1880s, though no manuscripts survive to confirm this. According to Lady Elgar's diary of 7 June 1907, 'Edward's head has been *full* of music ever since his return [from North America] and he has been continuously sketching & playing. He has sent Messrs. N[ovello] 2 lovely Motetts...' (Moore 1987: 672) Indeed, Elgar had sent the two motets to Alfred Littleton of Novello on 24 May:

> By this post I am sending to Wardour St two little things from the old sketches & Church things: they *may* do to go with the tiny 'Ave verum' but the editor must decide: the 'Cantiones Sacrae' is what I mean. They are tender little plants so treat them kindly whatever is their fate. (Moore 1987: 671)

Elgar's affection for his boyhood music is further reflected in the dedication to the wife of his oldest Worcester friend, Leicester. On 20 June 1907 Leicester wrote to the composer, acknowledging the dedication:

> You cannot realize how pleased my wife was at your kind thought of her, & you know that I am more than pleased...It is also a pleasure to know that you have published some of those early pieces.
> The farther we travel from the old days & the old associations the dearer they become. There must be many pieces among your 'archives' that would, if published, be hailed with delight by the Catholics.

Perhaps Elgar's reminiscent mood may have been due to his approaching fiftieth birthday. On 28 May he wrote to Jaeger:

EDWARD ELGAR: SACRED MUSIC

> I shall be fifty next week they tell me, but I don't know it: I have my pipe & the bicycle & a heavenly country to ride in — so an end. I take no interest whatever in music & just edit a few old boyish M.S.S. — music is off. (Moore 1987: 672)

These early church pieces were not the only 'boyish' sketches he was working on: he was revising the earliest music of all and shaping it into *The Wand of Youth* Suites. On 30 June Elgar wrote to Alfred Littleton: 'I have returned revises of the two little Latin things & with them two adaptations (in anthem-wise) with English words. I hope you will approve' (Moore 1987: 674). The *Ave Maris Stella*, dedicated to Charles Vincent Dolman, the parish priest of St Francis Xavier which Elgar attended while he lived at Hereford (1904-1911), appeared in English as *Jesu, meek and lowly*, the text by the Revd Henry Collins. There was a curious absence of reviews of the Op. 2 motets either in 1902 or 1907, particularly strange in view of Elgar's popularity and the fact that not even the *Musical Times* (a Novello publication) noticed them. Perhaps Latin texts were still considered provocative.

Both pieces are short but thoughtfully constructed. The *Ave Maria* is dominated by a single, recurring *berceuse*-like motif, full of that grace and wonderment that pervades Elgar's children's music. The *Ave Maris Stella*, very symmetrical in form, is similarly dominated by a flowing, looping motif; that it bears a resemblance to a section of the *Ave Verum* further suggests that it, too, dates from c. 1887. Even in Elgar's early, less chromatic music, he still succeeded in introducing some unexpected harmonic shifts. One of his fingerprints consisted of a chord, always simple, 'escaping' from the prevailing tonality and giving his music what Diana McVeagh describes as a 'shy' quality (McVeagh: 200). An early example occurs in the *Ave Maris Stella*, where a cadence in A minor (the supertonic) is deflected to a first inversion chord of G major:

Example 13: 'Ave Maris Stella', bars 27-30:

[musical notation]

This was a device which Elgar continued to exploit in his mature works, the Violin Concerto (1910-12) for example:

Example 14: Violin Concerto, 3rd movement, bars 76-77:

[musical notation]

1887 was eventful. Elgar played in the first Birmingham performance of Verdi's Requiem and attended the first performance in England of Bruckner's Seventh Symphony. That September he played in the Worcester Festival orchestra. Elgar was also in demand as a conductor and soloist, but the remuneration was meagre. He had already been supplementing his earnings by teaching the violin, piano accompaniment, and theory — mostly to young Malvern ladies — when a new pupil, Miss Caroline Alice

Roberts, enrolled in October 1886. Before long the Roberts's coachman was heard to say he 'thought there was more in it than the music lessons...' (Moore 1984a: 115). At the end of May 1887 Alice's mother, Lady Roberts died, and in response Elgar lent Alice (not yet a Catholic) Newman's *Dream of Gerontius*. She was now free of her daughterly responsibilities, and busied herself with her writing. Soon their respective interests in music and poetry overlapped: in 1888 Elgar set a poem of hers for the first time (one written eight years previously) in his song *The Wind at Dawn*. That July he completed *Liebesgrüss* — later to bring him fame but little fortune under the title *Salut d'amour* — and two months later he added the dedication to 'C.A. Roberts'. On 22 September they became engaged.

Perhaps it is not without significance that his next church piece, *Ecce Sacerdos Magnus* (Appendix One: 1.41), should be one of the clearest indicators of his mature style. It was written for a visit to the church on 9 October 1888 by Bishop Illsley, the Roman Catholic Archbishop of Birmingham. Elgar's sense of occasion is apparent here for the first time; it might almost be labelled his first ceremonial work. Besides the overall feeling of dignity, the stately rhythm of the organ pedal seems designed to accompany the Bishop's progress.

Referring to the service, Elgar wrote to his friend Charles Buck: 'Some special things had to be written for which we had no music' (Kennedy: 39). Clearly, he was under considerable pressure at the time:

> ...I had to set to work & compose it all & copy out the parts! Had to get it in anyhow & broke my neck doing it. Anyway the leading paper says the new composition was 'exquisite' so I suppose 'twas good enough. (Kennedy: 39)

Two manuscripts survive, but there is no trace of the original vocal score. A copy of the alto and tenor parts only, in Hubert Leicester's hand and dated 11 April 1890 is now preserved in the Jesuit Archives (Source A), but a second source contains the full score and instrumental parts of an orchestration of the motet in the composer's own hand.

This was made for a performance in November 1893 at the

dedication of a new chancel at St Catherine of Siena, Birmingham. *Ecce sacerdos* was published by Cary in 1889, and inscribed to Hubert Leicester, to whom Elgar wrote on 19 July of that year:

> By this post I send you an early copy of 'Ecce &c.'. I forget whether I asked your permission to gratify myself by putting your name at the commencement: if not I am sorry, & hope you will not mind: perhaps it will please you as a memento of the old days.

In spite of the limitations inherent in writing music for a church choir, Elgar was still able to experiment with tone colour. There is a wide variety of textures in the short, 53 bar piece. The composer is thematically concise: virtually every note can be traced to two alternating themes. Although the opening motive may seem typical of the composer in its broadness, Elgar probably had a theme from the Benedictus of Haydn's *Harmoniemesse* in mind when he composed the motet. It is even possible that he based his motet on it deliberately and that the Haydn Mass was sung at the same service for which *Ecce Sacerdos* was composed. The similarity extends beyond the melody line alone, as it will be seen that Elgar modelled some of his bass line on his Haydn, too:

Example 15 (a): Haydn 'Harmoniemesse', Benedictus, bars 1-3:

Example 15 (b): Elgar 'Ecce Sacerdos', bars 3-6:

Ecce Sacerdos was Elgar's last composition before he left St George's. He played for his final service there just one week before his marriage to Alice at the Brompton Oratory on 8 May 1889.

2. 1889-1910

After Elgar left St George's in 1889, church music ceased to be an important part of his output. He had been painfully aware of its limitations, but not having had the opportunities to develop his compositional skills elsewhere, he found the church an ideal place in which to serve his apprenticeship. His long struggles, however, were far from over. English music was emerging, very slowly, from its so-called 'dark age'. Elgar took what was the only option available to him, to progress slowly through the Festival system, writing large-scale choral works which he was to dismiss, late in life to Delius, as 'the penalty of my English environment' (Fenby: 124).

His progression took him through the social system, too. As the son of a shopkeeper in Victorian England, Elgar was subject to suffocating prejudice, heightened by his Catholicism. Later in life Elgar talked to his friend Rosa Burley of the resentment he felt:

> He replied that I little knew how seriously his career had been hampered by his Catholicism. He told me of post after post which would have been open to him but for the prejudice against his religion, of golden opportunities snatched from his grasp by inferior men of more acceptable views. It was a subject on which he evidently felt very bitter for he embroidered it at great length. (Burley and Carruthers: 26)

Rosa Burley went on to recall how

> he felt himself branded as something very like a social pariah....His work as a musician inevitably brought him into contact with people who were as much his superiors

socially as they were his inferiors aesthetically, and their
easy manners and scarcely veiled contempt caused him a
misery and resentment from which he never wholly shook
himself free. (Burley and Carruthers: 45)

The Elgars' sensitivity to the subject is also revealed in correspondence with F.G. Edwards, the editor of the *Musical Times*, who was preparing an article on the composer to appear at the time of the *Gerontius* premiere. Alice had worked through the galleys, and in her letter commented on the Elgar Brothers shop:

As E. has *nothing* to do with the business in Worcester
would you please leave out details which do not affect him
& with which he has nothing to do — His interests being
quite unconnected with business. (Moore 1984a: 326)

Elgar added a note of his own:

Now — as to the whole 'shop' episode — I don't care a d--n!
I know it has ruined me & made life impossible until I what
you call made a name — I know I was kept out of everything decent, 'cos 'his father keeps a shop'. (Moore 1984a:
326-7)

Even in his domestic life Elgar felt this bigotry — from Caroline Alice Roberts's family (her parents were dead), who thought she was marrying below her station: he, a penniless local musician, was the son of a local tradesman, and she was the daughter of a military man who had distinguished himself in India and retired as Major-General Sir Henry Gee Roberts. Miss Roberts's maternal grandfather was none other than Robert Raikes, a leading light in the establishment of Anglican Sunday Schools, so in the Roberts's eyes Elgar's religion was a further black mark against him. The effect on Elgar of such narrow-mindedness manifested itself in his seesawing emotions for the rest of his life, in the swings from haughty detachment to bouts of raging and at times self-pitying depression which puzzled so many who came into contact with him. His hypersensitivity never left him. As late as 1921, when he had enjoyed great acclaim, he wrote to Sidney Colvin that 'as a child and as a young man and as a mature man no single person was ever kind to me' (De-la-Noy: 191).

Right from the beginning, though, the new Mr and Mrs Elgar attempted to break away from it all. After their honeymoon at Ventnor on the Isle of Wight in May 1899, they moved straight to London in search of a new start. In Upper Norwood they were conveniently close to the Crystal Palace, and August Manns remained supportive, programming pieces of Elgar's from time to time. But for Elgar it was to be a long struggle: much of his energy was devoted to visiting West End publishers. Several of his manuscripts were accepted, among them the *Vesper Voluntaries* for organ, the part song *My Love dwelt in a Northern Land*, and piano and violin pieces, including *Salut d'Amour*. The capital's musical attractions compensated in some measure for his frustrations: among the many concerts and operas he heard was a performance in the first London run of Verdi's *Otello*.

Throughout a depressing winter, Elgar battled with ill health. At the end of the year came the good news that Alice was pregnant, and a daughter, who they named Carice, was born on 14 August 1890. She was baptized a Catholic on 2 September. (The baby's nurse agreed to attend the Catholic ceremony only so long as she did not have to bow down to any images [Young: 1978: 110].) In what was otherwise an unhappy period musically, a commission for an orchestral work for the 1890 Three Choirs Festival at Worcester raised Elgar's spirits, and he composed the first of his concert overtures, *Froissart*. All the time Elgar remained in touch with the Leicester family and welcomed news of his old church. In June he had written a Litany for them (see p.45); two months later, Hubert Leicester wrote on 22 August reporting on the music: 'We have just come from Church, it is a "special" day...Music — "Kalliwoda"[.] To-night we are to have one of your "Litanies" & Righini's "Tantum", & Mendelssohn's "Magnificat"'.

Elgar soon realised how valuable his contacts in provincial Worcester were, and increasing financial pressures led him to begin regular trips to Malvern to teach, an occupation he described for his first biographer as 'like turning a grindstone with a dislocated shoulder' (Buckley: 43). As he reported to his friend Frank Webb in February: 'The winter has been truly awful: the fogs here are terrifying & make me very ill: yesterday all day & to-day until two o'clock we have been in a sort of yellow darkness: I groped my way to church this morning & returned in an hour's time a weird and blackened thing with a great & giddy headache' (Moore 1989: 36). That church could have been one of many: during their time in London the Elgars attended a variety, including St Mary's in Chelsea, Our Lady of Victories in Kensington (pro-cathedral in pre-Westminster Cathedral days), the Carmelite church, Brook Green, Farm St, even St Dominic's in Haverstock Hill (Hodgkin: 4). The winter of 1890-1 brought renewed ill-health and depression. The family resolved to return to Worcestershire, and settled the following May in a house named 'Forli' (after the medieval Italian painter of angelic musicians) in Malvern Link. There composition flourished. In May 1892 Elgar completed the *Serenade* for Strings, now justly celebrated as one of his loveliest works, but then rejected by Novello as 'very good' but 'practically unsaleable' (Moore 1987: 10). Such experiences heightened Elgar's realization that he would have to produce the sort of large-scale choral works that were in vogue at the time. A trip to Germany in August 1892, which included visits to Beethoven's birthplace at Bonn, Bayreuth (to hear *Die Meistersinger, Tristan und Isolde,* and *Parsifal* twice), and Heidelberg (where the party heard Mascagni's newly-composed *Cavalleria rusticana*), gave Elgar the inspiration to complete his first big choral work, *The Black Knight.* Elgar described it as a 'Symphony for Chorus and Orchestra founded upon Uhland's poem "Der schwarze Ritter"', and though the libretto, a translation from the German by Longfellow, is poor, the premiere in Worcester on 18 April 1893 revealed a cosmopolitan score with little trace of English parochialism. Elgar was coming increasingly under the spell of Wagner, and later that year he, with Alice and friends, paid another visit to Germany, where at Munich they heard the *Ring* complete, *Tannhäuser, Die Meistersinger, Tristan,* and even *Die Feen*. Reluctantly, Elgar returned to Worcester in time to play in the Festival orchestra. In Bavaria, predominantly Catholic, Elgar felt a freedom he missed in England. He made clear its attractions in a letter written to his nieces and nephews, the Grafton children, in August 1892:

> Now this is so different to England because it is a Catholic country and in this part there are no Protestants: & the church is open all day & you see workmen & workwomen

carrying their rosaries & they go into the church as they pass by & say a few prayers (like you do without going to church) & go on with their work. & then during mass at the elevation they ring one of the great bells in the church tower & all the people in the street know it is the elevation & take off their hats & make the sign of the cross! on the roads here are crucifixes very often & generally a few trees planted round them for shade & people passing by stay & say a prayer & rest and then go on their way. (Hodgkin: 4)

On each trip to Germany Elgar had been searching for church music suitable for Hubert Leicester to use at St George's. Of the first journey he reported to Leicester from Lindau on 10 August 1892:

> We are this far on our way home after having been far into the wilds of the Algäuer Alps in South Bavaria. Now, Bavaria being a Catholic country I have kept a sharp look out for Church Music. At Obertsdorf, a little place in the mountains I heard a good Mass done by the villagers, very well conducted by the schoolmaster with whom I subsequently became acquent: he let me look over their stock & I made notes thereon.
>
> I was sorry to find that the Mass I heard is only obtainable in *separate* parts: i.e. organ pt., *vocal pts* & instrumental parts all *separate* — no score of any kind — so that would not be of any use: it was written by a man in Augsburg & was very nice. In addition to the organ they had a Hautboy, Clarinet, Violin & a Trombone: the last made a ghastly noise.
>
> Now, I would not have bothered you with all this only to say amongst the other masses shewn to me I have made a note of several which I should like: they are, apparently, about the difficulty of F. Turner's mass, but more musicianly. No display & no flourishes, but plain, nicely harmonised music...
>
> There was a requiem but that was Gregorian & the other things were much as usual: nowhere else I heard anything worthy of note: next Sunday we hope to be in Cologne on our way home but I expect there the music will be too elaborate to be useful.

And after the 1894 visit, Leicester wrote to Elgar: 'Pray accept our very best thanks for the beautiful Crucifix you so kindly brought us on your return from Germany. It is indeed a treasure especially considering where & from whom it was bought & by one who did not forget us when so far from home'.

1894 was not a prolific year for Elgar, though he did turn out his ceremonial *Sursum Corda* (for strings, brass and organ) for the visit in April to Worcester Cathedral of the Duke of York, the future George V. Three months later, at St George's, Alice was received into the Roman Catholic Church by Father Knight, from whom she had been taking instruction.

In spite of the success of the *Sursam Corda*, Elgar was still very much cast as a 'local' musician: that summer he arranged the Good Friday Music from *Parsifal* for a Matinée Musicale at Worcester Girls' High School. About this time he contemplated a large-scale religious work based on St Augustine's *Civitas Dei*. He even had a libretto prepared, but as Moore has commented (Moore 1984a: 183), 'such an ultimate division of good from evil needed a personal security that was beyond Edward and the art that reflected him then'. Instead, he began thinking about what would become his next big choral work, *Scenes from the Saga of King Olaf*. The hero of the saga had fascinated Elgar as a child, and when in 1895 a commission came for a big choral work for the North Staffordshire Festival the following year, he attacked his work with renewed energy. There were other distractions, though. In mid-1895 he produced his first large abstract work, the Organ Sonata No. 1 for his friend Hugh Blair, the organist of Worcester Cathedral, to play for a visiting group of American organists on 8 July. Elgar's note in the manuscript, 'one week's work', was only a slight exaggeration, and the date, 3 July, indicates why Blair had insufficient time to master its difficulties. The composer's friend Rosa Burley was present at the performance and suggested in her headmistressy fashion that Blair's 'performance of the Sonata showed that he had either not learned it or else had celebrated the event unwisely' (Burley: 86). Elgar got away from it all by going on holiday to Garmisch. That year he completed the *Scenes from the Bavarian Highlands*, set to Alice's words.

Just weeks before the premiere of *King Olaf* came the first performance of what was to remain Elgar's biggest Three Choirs commission. *The Light of Life*, which the composer himself conducted at Worcester on 10 September 1896, was the only religious oratorio he wrote during this period. Elgar's preferred name for the work was *Lux Christi*, but since the premiere was scheduled for an Anglican cathedral and Latin was considered provocative to the Protestant public the oratorio was published under the English title. (As it was, the former Precentor of Worcester Cathedral, Edward Vine Hall, successfully raised an objection to lines which struck him as 'absolutely irrelevant': 'Hadst Thou a son, O Lord, how could'st Thou bear/To see him made Thy curse?'. Elgar's correspondence with the publishers over the change is printed in Moore 1987: 36-39.) The libretto, by the Rev. E. Capel-Cure, is based on the healing of the blind man related in St John's gospel. Although the work is conventional in many respects, it reveals the seeds of several ideas which Elgar developed later. There were, however, some compromises, like a fugal section of which Elgar said: 'I thought a fugue would be expected of me. The British public would hardly tolerate oratorio without a fugue.' Showing a certain detachment, he added: 'I hope there's enough counterpoint to give the real British religious respectability' (Buckley: 31). Elgar, who frequently pretended autodidactic ignorance, must have enjoyed setting his clever little fugue to 'The wisdom of their wise men shall perish'.

Perhaps it is significant that both *King Olaf* and *The Light of Life* have protagonists who suffer isolation for their beliefs. In *Olaf* it is a Christian king whose challenge is to convert a pagan country; in the oratorio, the blind man is ostracised by the Pharisees for his faith in Christ. A comparison of *King Olaf* and *The Light of Life* shows the extent to which the English oratorio tradition cramped Elgar's style: the secular work is by far the more original and inspired. Both *The Light of Life* and *King Olaf* were enthusiastically received, and Elgar began to enjoy a level of success with the public that he could only have dreamed of a few years earlier. *The Black Knight* and *King Olaf* were taken up by choral societies up and down the country, and special presentation copies of *King Olaf* were even made for the Kings of Sweden and Norway. Indeed, 1897 was a year of royal associations: Queen Victoria's Diamond Jubilee brought the first glimpse of Elgar the national composer, with the *Imperial March* and his cantata *The Banner of St George*. The irony, that St George — patron saint of Elgar's old church — originally a Catholic saint, now guarded a Protestant country, could not have been lost on Elgar.

Elgar's commission for the Three Choirs Festival that year, the *Te Deum and Benedictus* (Appendix One: 2.1), was the first piece of church music (the small Litany chant excepted) he had written since leaving his post at St George's eight years before. It was composed for the opening service of the Festival at Hereford on 12 September 1897. The setting was dedicated to Dr George Robertson Sinclair (1863-1917), the organist of Hereford Cathedral (whose bulldog, Dan, Elgar immortalized in the 'Enigma' Variations two years later), who conducted the premiere. Percy Hull, Sinclair's assistant organist at Hereford, was present when Elgar visited Sinclair on 5 June 1897 and played from his sketches. Hull recalled:

> He was as nervous as a kitten and heaved a huge sigh of relief when Sinclair said: 'It is *very very* modern, but I think it will do; you shall play it again after supper when Hull and I will give you our final verdict.' All this in Sinclair's stammering and somewhat patronising fashion. ('Elgar at Hereford' in *The RAM Magazine*, 1960; quoted in Moore 1984a: 223)

Sinclair was not alone in finding it 'modern'. Commentary written a few years after the premiere suggests that opinion on the work remained divided:

> It may be argued that the music is not church music, that it is not English music, that it is not good music. To all or any of these charges one might listen with patience and due show of respect...But it could never be maintained that there was a 'Te Deum' of like mood and feeling. The introduction is calculated to startle good men and true whose standard is found in the work of English church musicians. The very phrasing of the words is new and alarming. There is, however, much delicious music, full enjoyment of which comes to many only after a struggle with prepossessions. (Buckley: 52)

During May and June 1897 Elgar worked hard at the *Te Deum*

and Benedictus in order to have it ready for chorus rehearsals. He dispatched the work to Novello on 15 June; the publishers offered him fifteen guineas, which he accepted in a letter dated 26 June (Moore 1987: 48).

Perhaps the most significant outcome of the composition of the *Te Deum and Benedictus* was that it brought Elgar into personal contact with August Johannes Jaeger, a German who was employed at Novello as a music editor. Jaeger immediately recognized Elgar's superiority over the composers of part-songs and church cantatas upon which Novello largely relied. When Elgar completed the orchestration at 'Forli', Malvern, on 31 July, he sent it to the publishers and received an encouraging response from Jaeger. On 4 August, Alice Elgar noted in her diary: 'E. heard from Mr Jaeger — quite as enthusiastic as he shd. be over E's music for Hereford' (Moore 1987: 48). This prompted an appreciative reply from Elgar:

> You praise my new work too much — but you understand it; — when it is performed will anyone say *any*thing different from what they wd. say over a commercial brutality like the 'Flag of England' [composed by Frederick Bridge to words by Rudyard Kipling in 1897] for instance: naturally no one will & the thing dies & so do I —
> All the same hearty thanks for your sympathy: I told you that I wd. never put pen to paper when I had finished this work: but shall I? (Moore 1987: 49)

This was answered with another letter of encouragement which evidently made some reference to the inadequate fee of fifteen guineas. Elgar replied on 6 August:

> I must send one line to thank you for your last letter which has put new heart into me!....
> ....please do not think I am a disappointed person, either commercially or artistically — what I feel is the utter want of *sympathy* — they[,] i.e. principally music critics, lump me with people I abhor — mechanics. Now my music, such as it is, is alive, you say it has heart — I always say to my wife (over any piece or passage of my work that pleases me): 'if you cut that it would bleed!' *You* seem to see that — but who else does? (Moore 1987: 49-50)

EDWARD ELGAR: SACRED MUSIC

After a short break in Germany, where Elgar heard Richard Strauss conduct *Tristan und Isolde* in Munich that August, he returned to England in time for the *Te Deum*'s first performance. Elgar sat in the organ loft of Hereford Cathedral. One of those present in the congregation was Jaeger, who wrote to the composer on 15 September:

> I travelled from Huddersfield to London *via Hereford* for the express purpose of hearing your splendid work, & was well rewarded for my 'pains'. All my anticipations were realized & more than realized, & this though the performance in my opinion was by no means *perfect*...I *have* heard your finest, most spontaneous & most deeply felt & most effective work & I was *very* happy. (Moore 1987: 50-51)

Elgar appreciated the fact that Jaeger was German, and the two men had in common that they were both outsiders in the English musical establishment. Clearly, Jaeger was championing Elgar's work:

> Well, the Papers *are* good, *some* of them, while others, like the 'Pall Mall' talk a load of *Rubbish*. Bennett [in *The Daily Telegraph*] is good & Herbert Thompson (*Yorkshire Post*): I spoke to the latter after the Service & gave him a 'piece of my mind' in re your work, and he seemed to be largely agreed with me. Don't laugh when I add that I consider him of the best, most wideawake & *competent* critics in England.
>   You see I am conceited enough to think that I too can appreciate a good thing & see genius in musicians who are *not* yet dead, or even not yet well known, or Cathedral Organists or directors of Schools of music in Colleges for Boys! This by the way.
>   ....The critics don't lay half enough stress on the *feeling* in the music, the emotional qualities which *alone* make music *live*. Our Editor & other good folk keep on saying '*Very* clever, *very* clever' &c &c & I say: *hang* your cleverness, *that* won't make *any* music great & 'alive'! *Emotional* qualities *never* seem to concern our Editor. (Moore 1987: 51)

Elgar included an enigmatic note under his signature in the orchestral score, 'Inter spem et metum', which translates as 'Between

1. The earliest known photograph of Elgar, with his mother, c. 1859

2. Elgar aged 14, about the time he first played for a mass at St George's

3. The wind quartet: Frank Exton and Frank Elgar (seated); William Leicester, Edward Elgar,

4. Elgar in his twenties

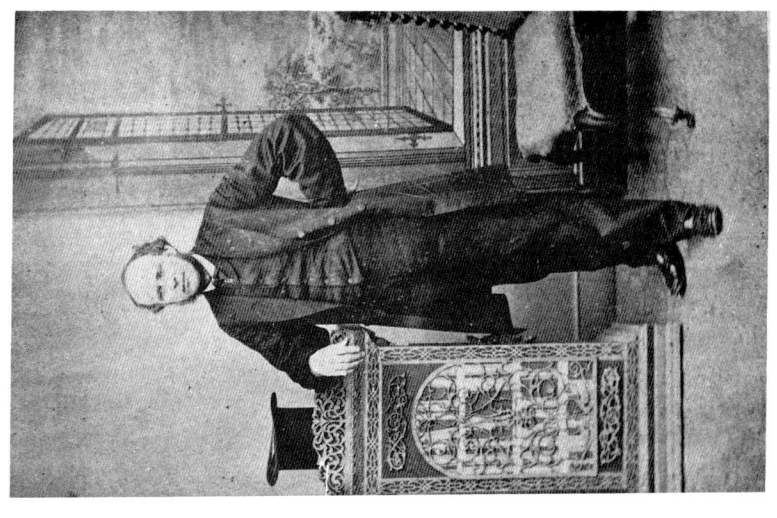

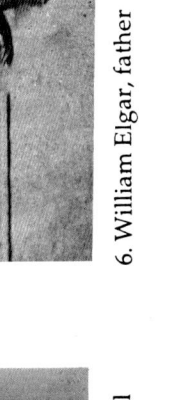

5. William Dove, organist of Worcester Cathedral during Elgar's youth

6. William Elgar, father

7. St George's Catholic Church, Worcester

8. Interior of St George's

9. Worcester High Street in the nineteenth century, with the Elgar Brothers music shop at No. 10 on the left

10. Ivan Kramskoy's 'The Temptation of Christ', which hung in Elgar's study

11. Edward and Alice Elgar

12. Hubert Leicester

S. GEORGE'S CATHOLIC CHURCH,
WORCESTER.

The Clergy of S. George's Catholic Church, Worcester, respectfully invite _____ on Sunday, June 6th, to the Solemn opening of the New Chancel of the Church.

High Mass at 11 o'clock, Sermon by the Right Rev. Dr. Ullathorne, O.S.B., Bishop of Birmingham.

Vespers and Benediction 6.30. p.m., Sermon by the Rev. W. Humphrey, S.J.

MUSIC:

Hummell's Mass in B flat, (with Orchestral Accompaniment.)
Offertory.—Instrumental.
Domine salvam fac .... E. W. ELGAR.

Vespers B.V.M. ...... (Lauda Jerusalem—ANFOSSI, Accompanied)
Magnificat ....
Salve Regina .... E. W. ELGAR.
Sanctum et terribile. .... PERGOLESI.
O Salutaris .... GLOVER.
Agnus Dei .... HAYDN, No. 2.
Tantum Ergo .... E. W. ELGAR.
Domine salvam fac.

Organist—Mr. W. H. Elgar. Leader—Mr. E. W. Elgar.

A Collection will be made at each Service for the Restoration Fund.

N.B.—Father Humphrey will preach both Morning and Evening on Sunday, June 13th.

May 26th, 1880.

St. George's Catholic Choir.

RULES.

1. —No person can join the Choir until his or her name has been submitted to the Priest in charge of the Mission and approved by him. Each Member must also satisfy the Organist of his or her musical fitness, sign the Rules, and promise to conform thereto.

2. —The Choirmaster shall be appointed by the Priest in charge of the Mission, to whom he shall be responsible for the proper conduct of the Choir, and the musical portion of the Services.

3. —All Members to attend the 11 o'clock Mass and the Evening Service on Sundays, also the weekly Rehearsal, and to be in their places, which shall be arranged by the Choirmaster, not later than five minutes before the time appointed for the commencement of the Service or Rehearsal. Members who may be compelled from special causes to be absent at any of these times, shall give notice of such intention to the Choirmaster as early as possible, and not later than fifteen minutes before the time appointed for the commencement of the Service or Rehearsal.

4. —The Members to conform in all Musical matters to the instruction of the Organist, whose authority on all questions of Music shall be supreme; each Member must sing the part assigned to him or her by the Choirmaster or the Organist, and in no way interfere with the other Members of the Choir.

5. —The greatest decorum to be observed in the Choir on all occasions, and no conversation carried on.

6. —No person (other than the members) to be allowed in the Choir, without the consent of the Choirmaster.

7. —All Music belonging to the Choir to be under the care of the Choirmaster, and no Music to be taken away without his consent, and until a memorandum shall have been made of the same.

8. —Any person damaging or losing a piece of Music shall make the same good.

9. —The Music to be performed on each Sunday shall, as far as practicable, be arranged at the weekly Rehearsal, and practised, unless thoroughly known, by all the Members. The various books to be upon the stands before the commencement of each Service.

10. —A Rehearsal of at least one hour's duration, shall be held every week.

It being a great honour to be allowed to take an active part in the musical portion of the Divine Service, and as the want of interest of any one Member will greatly hinder the progress of the Choir, it is hoped that all will cheerfully make such little sacrifices as may be required to carry out the Rules.

I have read these Rules and give them my full approbation.

J. FOXWELL, S.J.

CONDITIONS OF MEMBERSHIP.

I hereby promise to conform to the foregoing Rules, and will use my best endeavours to promote the efficiency of Saint George's Catholic Choir.

Carroll Gear
Aug 29, 1886

St. George's Catholic Choir.

In order to put the Choir on a satisfactory footing, and to ensure regular and punctual attendance at the Services and Rehearsals, we find it necessary to request you to sign the enclosed Conditions of Membership and return the same to the Choirmaster, before the end of the present month, if you wish to remain a Member.

EDWARD ELGAR, *Organist.*

HUBERT LEICESTER, *Choirmaster.*

Feast of the Assumption, 1886.

---

14. Rules drawn up by Elgar and Hubert Leicester in 1886, to put the St George's Catholic choir on 'a satisfactory footing'

hope and fear'. Perhaps he was referring to the trouble over the Catholicity of his oratorio *Lux Christi* at the previous year's Festival.

The *Te Deum and Benedictus* blended stylistic elements of English church music with features of Elgar's early works written for St George's. Scored for chorus (SATB) and organ or orchestra, it was his largest church setting yet and turned out to be the longest he would ever write. The considerable chromaticism of the piece shocked people who were accustomed to the mundane church settings of the time. As the critic of the *Morning Post* put it, 'For the most part the music indeed is more suggestive of a warlike song of triumph than an expression of Christian praise and prayer'.

Of all Elgar's mature church works, it is the most overtly Anglican, and many passages suggest that Elgar was playing to the gallery. Certainly it fails to reach the levels Elgar had even then set for himself. Because the text is difficult to cast in a particular formal scheme (unless each verse is given a movement to itself, in the manner of longer settings by Handel and others), Elgar achieves a sense of unity through the development of his opening pair of themes, to which much of the music may be traced. The characteristic Elgarian falling seventh appears frequently, right from the very first bar. Strong triplets dominate the more affirmative moments. The triplet figure, which was also to become one of Elgar's hallmarks, began to feature in his music during the 1890s with *The Black Knight*; but it is prominent in boyhood favourites of Elgar's, such as the Overture to *Tannhäuser* and the Coronation March from Meyerbeer's *Le prophète*. Ripe sequences give shape to the *Te Deum* and return in recapitulation in the closing 'Gloria'. In between comes the lyrical *Benedictus* (in a flowing 12/8), lightly accompanied. Whatever the work's shortcomings, perhaps it is worth remembering that only ten years earlier Elgar had written the *Pie Jesu* (whose style some of the more diatonic passages in the 1897 work reflect). The 1890s were years of great technical advance for Elgar, and his music from this decade reflects a high degree of eclecticism. Perhaps it is not surprising that the *Te Deum and Benedictus* should reflect Elgar's wide musical horizons, most notably the influence of Wagner. As Peter Dennison has pointed out (Dennison: 102), one passage bears a striking resemblance to a phrase in 'Am stillen Herd' in *Die Meistersinger*, Act 1, Scene 3:

Example 16 (a): Elgar 'Te Deum', bars 157-160:

Example 16 (b): Wagner, 'Die Meistersinger', bars 1497-1498:

Elgar had seen the opera several times since the 1880s, and in his score he noted 'schön' against these particular bars.

After the Three Choirs Festival, Elgar contemplated a choral work for the following year's Leeds Festival on the subject of 'The Flight into Egypt'. Soon his mind turned to St Augustine and the conversion of Britain, but he abandoned those thoughts too, perhaps because the subject might have been considered too Catholic for Leeds.

For Christmas that year Elgar designed a private Christmas card with his simple setting of the words 'Grete Malverne on a rocke' (a facsimile of the card appears facing p. 44 in Young 1965). Years later Elgar set the unaccompanied four-part music to a different carol, 'Lo! Christ the Lord is born' (Appendix One: 2.2), by Shapcott Wensley (the librettist of *The Banner of St George*). The idea originated with Jaeger, who would have received the original card: owing to ill-health Jaeger had been forced to leave Novello, and it was from his sickbed that he wrote to his old firm on 3 November 1908 suggesting that they should publish the piece. In due course, and after consultation with Elgar, it was published as a 'Carol for

Christmastide' in 1909. The music is vigorous but unpretentious. Although it is set in F major, many lines end with minor chords, evoking a modal feel.

Queen Victoria was the dedicatee of his next big choral work, *Caractacus*. There is a strong patriotic feeling in the finale, where, in a curious jingoistic twist, the victorious Romans sing of the day when their empire will be replaced by that of the British. Elgar defended the patriotism in a letter to Jaeger: 'I *did* suggest that we should dabble in patriotism in the Finale, when lo! the "worder" (that's good) instead of merely paddling his feet goes and gets naked and wallows in it' (Moore 1984a: 239). But Elgar's real inspiration was his beloved Malvern Hills where most of the action is set. Much of the music was composed at Birchwood Lodge, a summer cottage that he had taken near Malvern.

Caractacus had its first performance at the Leeds Festival on 5 October 1898. Only days later, Elgar revealed to Jaeger that he was at work on a set of variations. The great conductor Hans Richter took charge of the 'Enigma' Variations at the St James's Hall premiere on 19 June 1899, a performance that brought Elgar his biggest success yet. But there were distractions and other music on his mind, too. The Elgars had moved from 'Forli' to a house in Malvern which they named 'Craeg Lea' (an anagram of the family's initials and surname, C, A, & E ELGAR) and the composer was busily completing his song cycle *Sea Pictures* for Clara Butt to sing at the Norwich Festival that year. Also, as he confided to Jaeger, he was 'to do the principal novelty for Birmingham' the following year.

For Elgar 1900 began promisingly, with the visit on New Year's Day of the chairman of the Birmingham Festival, G.H. Johnstone, to discuss plans for that year's commission, *The Dream of Gerontius*. A copy of Cardinal Newman's poem (1865) about the journey of a man's soul from death to his arrival before God had been a wedding present to the Elgars from Father Knight of St George's, Worcester. The subject had been on Elgar's mind since then (though he had known the poem even before his marriage), at one stage in the guise of a 'Gordon' symphony, after the national hero who met his death in Khartoum having just discovered Newman's poem. For someone who claimed to have suffered because of his Catholicism, setting *Gerontius* was a bold statement, perhaps even an act of defiance. It contained hardly any Scripture to soothe the Protestants who made up the big choral societies, and much of the doctrine to which they objected. Elgar believed that Dvořák had been discouraged from setting the poem for the 1888 Birmingham Festival for these reasons, but in the event Johnstone raised no problems over its Catholicity. On 12 January Elgar went to the Birmingham Oratory to meet Father Neville, Cardinal Newman's executor, and was granted permission to adapt and shorten the poem for his libretto. The Birmingham Oratory had special significance for Elgar, since it was there that Newman had written *Gerontius*.

Now with a firm commission in hand he worked furiously. The mystical, meditative spirit of the poem touched Elgar as nothing else had, and at Birchwood Lodge on 3 August he completed *Gerontius*, adding to his score a quotation from Ruskin's *Sesame and Lilies*: 'This is the best of me; for the rest I ate, and drank, and slept, loved and hated, like another; my life was as the vapour, and is not; but *this* I saw and knew; this, if anything of mine, is worth your memory'.

Nothing in 'Anglican' works like *The Light of Life* and the *Te Deum and Benedictus* prepares one for *Gerontius's* greatness. Those Worcester Catholics who knew Elgar claimed that *Gerontius* embodied something of the old music from St George's, and that this background had left its mark on the work. There were indeed themes from Elgar's early experiences, or as the composer himself put it to Jaeger, from 'my insidest inside'. First, there was the quotation on the back of the old French engraving of the Death of St Joseph, given to the eleven-year-old Elgar by his parish priest (see p. 19). Other words would have brought up memories: Newman took lines for his text from the 'Bona mors' service, 'devotions for a good death' (notably 'Holy Mary, pray for him', and 'Be merciful, be gracious'), and Gerontius's long statement in Part I begins with the words of the Good Friday liturgy, 'Sanctus, Fortis, Sanctus Deus'. There are musical suggestions, too. Early on during composition, Elgar had written to Leicester (20 February 1900) hoping to trace some of the St George's music: 'Do you remember the old Blue cloth covered book — large 8vo. I think pubd. by Burns which used to be at the Church: an odd volume containing some Gregorian things (we did the Te Deum) & Benediction services[.] Wd. it be possible for me to see it?'. Elgar's simple setting of 'Be merciful' in Part I, and especially its return in Part II, suggests the flavour of his church writing; and the chant-like passage telling of how the prophets were rescued 'by Thy gracious power', and choral Amens resemble the music he had written in his early St George's days. In spite of these influences, Elgar was anxious not to let *Gerontius* sound like an overblown church work. When it came to the tenor in the title part, he preferred John Coates's interpretation, finding Gervase Elwes too 'other-worldly'. And he wrote to Jaeger on 28 August 1900:

> Look here: I imagined Gerontius to be a man like us, not a Priest or a Saint, but a *sinner*, a repentant one of course but still no end of a *wordly man* in his life, & now brought to book. Therefore I've not filled *his* part with Church tunes & rubbish but a good, healthy full-blooded romantic, remembered worldliness, so to speak. It is, I imagine, much more difficult to tear one's self away from a well to do world than from a cloister. (Moore 1987: 228)

Jaeger — an agnostic of Protestant upbringing — was full of praise for the work: 'Since "Parsifal" nothing of this mystic, religious kind of music has appeared to my knowledge that displays the same power and beauty as yours' (Moore 1984a: 306-7). In every page it is the work of someone who loved *Parsifal*, and yet it is unmistakably Elgar's own. *The Dream of Gerontius* had a special resonance for Catholics, but from most quarters its sentiments met with little sympathy, and its music proved to be beyond the comprehension and appreciation of the Birmingham forces and audience. Indeed, the form of *Gerontius* represented a dramatic break from convention: instead of separate numbers in the vein of Handel and Mendelssohn oratorios, Elgar fused aria, recitative, and chorus into a continuous stream of music, broken only at the transition between worlds. (The contrast of musical atmosphere between Parts I and II is striking.)

Not surprisingly, the premiere on 3 October was a fiasco. Elgar finished the work only two months before that date, and so allowed little time for chorus rehearsals. But the situation was made worse by circumstances out of his control. The chorus master, Charles Swinnerton Heap, had died and was replaced at short notice by W.C. Stockley, who was out of his depth in this music and by all accounts held anti-Catholic views. By the time Hans Richter took charge it was too late for him to weld it together. (Vaughan Williams recalled that at the premiere the tenor soloist sang his part 'like a Stainer anthem' [Moore 1984a: 331].) The critics' recognition of the work's stature offered the composer little consolation. The reception of *Gerontius* hurt Elgar deeply, and it brought on a terrible sense of despondency, worse than the composer had suffered in years. It also brought one of the earliest hints of the insecurity of his faith, as his letter to Jaeger of 9 October revealed:

> I have worked hard for the last forty years & at the last, Providence denies me a decent hearing of my work: so I submit — I always said God was against art & still believe it. anything [sic] obscene or trivial is blessed in this world & has a reward...I have allowed my heart to open once — it is now shut against every religious feeling and every soft, gentle impulse *for ever*. (Moore 1984a: 334)

Moore has observed that 'it showed how he had secretly used the inspiration of *Gerontius* as a wager against his own insecure faith' (Moore 1984a: 335). Whatever Elgar's private programme, *Gerontius* is religious at a level much deeper than conventional oratorios, and it is surely this that makes it his greatest work. Significantly, he never termed it an 'oratorio'.

Though 1900 ended in deep depression for Elgar, there were a few interludes to raise his spirits. On St Cecilia's Day, Cambridge University conferred an honorary Mus.D. on him, an honour only a few years previously bestowed on Tchaikovsky, Grieg, Saint-Saëns, and Bruch. Further encouragement came early in 1901, with the first performance in Germany of the 'Enigma' Variations, in Düsseldorf on 7 February under Julius Buths. The Germans were sympathetic to Elgar's music, and received *Gerontius* enthusiastically at the end of the year; after a second performance at the Lower Rhine Festival in 1902, Richard Strauss proposed his famous toast to 'the first English progressivist, Meister Edward Elgar', a compliment that did not go down well among all members of the English musical establishment. Indeed, the contrast could not have been greater with the parochialism of England, where a few months before *Gerontius* was due to be performed at the Worcester Three Choirs Festival in 1902, the festival committee raised the question of the 'propriety' of allowing a work so full of Roman Catholic theology to be performed in an Anglican cathedral. They proposed the substitution of 'Lord', 'Jesus', or 'Saviour' for 'Mary', 'souls' for 'souls in purgatory', and so forth.

Jaeger had forseen this in 1900. He warned Elgar on 14 June:

> There is a lot of *Joseph & Mary* about the work; very proper for a Roman Catholic lying at death's door to sing about, but likely to frighten *some* d--d fools of Protestants. I had a LONG talk to the Secretary of one of the big Glasgow Societies yesterday & showed him proofs & so generally enthused over the work that I *hope* he will strongly recommend 'Gerontius' to his Society. But *he at once*, on reading the words spoke of the 'Roman Catholic Element' being so prominent!! 'Tommy Rot' you say; *Ditto* Says I, who am rather an Agnostic than anything else. But alas!, one must deal with people as one finds them, & if, without Bowdlerising a superb poem one can remove Mary & Joseph to a more distant Background, it may not be a bad thing! (Moore 1987: 189)

Elgar replied:

> As to the Catholic side, of course it will frighten the low church party but the poem must on no account be touched! sacrilege and not to be thought of: them that don't like it can be damned in their own way — not ours. It's awfully curious the attitude (towards sacred things) of the narrow English mind.

Elgar had been defiant then, but now he was so anxious to have the work performed that he sanctioned the de-Romanizing of the text, having got the grudging consent of Cardinal Newman's executors. In gratitude he gave his manuscript full score to the Birmingham Oratory, inscribing it 'with the deepest reverence to the memory of Cardinal Newman whose poem I have had the honour to set to music'.

Meanwhile, composition continued apace. 1901 saw the appearance of a second concert overture, *Cockaigne*, and incidental music for W.B. Yeats's and George Moore's *Grania and Diarmid* at the Gaiety Theatre in Dublin. In October the first two *Pomp and Circumstance* Marches were premiered. The first, with its 'Land of Hope and Glory' theme, has gained nationalistic associations in spite of what Michael Kennedy has detected as 'a note of recessional', a view further supported in the 'Pomp and Circumstance' title itself, which comes from Othello's farewell to arms. Nevertheless, Elgar did tell Buckley that he saw a composer as 'a bard for the people. He ought to write a popular tune sometimes' (Buckley: 48). This is what the public heard, and Elgar's reputation as a national composer continued to grow, confirmation of it coming when he was asked to compose a *Coronation Ode* for celebrations marking Edward VII's coronation in 1902.

Aware of the King's liking for the trio theme in the first *Pomp and Circumstance* March, he incorporated a vocal setting of the tune into the *Coronation Ode*. Both its scheduled first performance on 30 June at Covent Garden and the Coronation service itself on 26 June were postponed due the King's sudden attack of appendicitis. In a show of bravado, Elgar appeard unconcerned when he wrote to Jaeger on 25 June: 'Don't, for heaven's sake, *sympathize* with me — I don't care a tinker's damn! It gives me three blessed sunny days in my own country (for which I thank God or the Devil) instead of stewing in town' (Moore 1987: 360). The eventual Coronation at Westminster Abbey on 9 August 1902 did however include a hymn by Elgar, 'O Mightiest of the mighty' (Appendix One: 2.3), set to words by the Revd S. Childs Clarke. It was published by Novello in 1902 in a collection entitled 'Eight Hymns with Tunes suitable for use at Services in celebration of the Coronation of King Edward VII, 1902'. Strangely, no mention of Elgar's hymn is made in the 'Form and Order' of the Coronation that was published in preparation for the service in June.

Elgar began work on the hymn in good time: the sketches are dated 3 January 1902. That day he wrote to Jaeger, indicating that he was writing the hymn under some protestation:

> ...The Hymn is all 'wrong' — hymns always are — look at the accents in the first lines — then the words pause at the end of the third line in every stanza *except* 2 which requires

> to go on at once — That's the reason I never write hymn tunes — they're so ghastly inartistic.
> I'll try.
> The horrible musical atmosphere I plunged into at once in this benighted country nearly suffocated me — I *wish* it had completely. (Moore 1987: 323)

In a footnote he added: 'I enclose a tune — there are 10,000 people [who] can do this sort of thing better than I can' (Moore 1987: 323).

By 9 January his thoughts had turned to the financial arrangements:

> As to the Hymn Tune I thought £10/10/- but as it's for a special occasion it may be worth less on that account — or more! (Moore 1987: 323)

When the publishers did settle on a fee, it was five guineas, half of what Elgar had suggested (Moore 1987: 339).

Elgar was understandably frustrated with attitudes to music in Britain; his recent visit to Germany, where, among other things, *The Dream of Gerontius* had been successfully received in Düsseldorf, could only have served to heighten these feelings. He had previously aired his views on the 'British Public' in a letter to Jaeger in June 1900, referring to the composition of *The Dream of Gerontius*:

> I'm so sick of the whole thing: 'cos why? 'Cos every ass I meet says: — 'I suppose' or 'I hope you're going to keep the old A[ncient] & M[odern] Tune for "Praise to the Holiest"!!!!!['] Blast the B[ritish] P[ublic] — they have no souls, hearts or minds worth a thought. (Moore 1987: 201)

It was several years before Elgar composed another piece of church music. But it is worth noting the existence of a sketch marked 'Anthem' (Appendix One: 2.4) in a sketch-book begun on 30 December 1902. Pieces on adjacent pages suggest that it dates from the early years of the century, but the sketch-book remained in use throughout his life, as fragments from major works, including *The Apostles*, *The Kingdom*, *The Music Makers*, and his operatic project *The Spanish Lady* indicate. This E flat major/C minor fragment was not incorporated into any of the later anthems, nor does it appear to have been used elsewhere. If it had been, Elgar would have marked it with a 'K' sign, or 'Koppid', to indicate that he had copied it elsewhere. As he explained in one of his sketch-books (BL Add MS 63153: f. 19v.):

> The ridiculous word 'Koppid' meant that I had copied it fairly enough for anyone to read: I used the word to prevent confusion with the word 'copied' which was used by the professional copyist denoting that he had made a correct & finished copy for the printer.

Elgar's mother died on 1 September 1902, and his youngest sister, Dot, who had cared for her mother, now sought to become a Dominican nun. It was perhaps these events that inspired the renewed depth of religious emotion reflected in Elgar's next major work, *The Apostles*. It was commissioned for the 1903 Birmingham Festival, whose authorities were apparently anxious to restore the festival's reputation after the fiasco of *Gerontius*. Elgar cited a remark made by his schoolmaster, Francis Reeves, as an influence on his choice of subject: 'The Apostles were poor men, young men... perhaps before the descent of the Holy Ghost not cleverer than some of you here' (Buckley: 8). This clearly made an impression on the young Elgar, and now it took him back to his youth. (In recognition of Reeves's influence, Elgar sent his old teacher an *Apostles* libretto when the work was finished.) His thoughts on an 'Apostles' theme as the basis for a work went back at least as far as 1899, when Elgar turned his attention to Judas as a possible subject — the outsider among the Apostles. He mentioned Judas to Jaeger in a letter on 18 November 1899: 'I'm glad you like my idea of Judas. I'll send yr. another wildly expressive bit but it's very hard to try and write *one's self* out & find that one's Soul is not *simple* enough for the British choral society' (Moore 1987: 153). In a sense, the character of Judas echoes Elgar's own feelings of hopelessness, desperation that the composer may have been fighting in composing the oratorios. Writing in 1903 to his friend Canon Gorton, Elgar said 'To my mind *Judas'* crime & sin was *despair*... In these days, when every "modern" person seems to think "suicide" is the natural way out of everything (Ibsen &c. &c.) my plan, if explained, may do some good' (Moore 1990:131). And in his 'Notes for an Article (sketch) on the Character of Judas Iscariot' (preserved at the Birthplace Museum), he wrote 'I [see in] Judas Iscariot a much more terrible "lesson" than the ordinary acceptation of his character by the unthinking, the unreading, and the invincibly ignorant allows'. He embroidered on the subject in his interview with the *Strand Magazine* in 1904:

> I was always particularly impressed with Archbishop Whately's conception of Judas, who, as he wrote, 'had no design to betray his Master to death, but to have been as confident of the will of Jesus to deliver Himself from His enemies by a miracle as He must have been certain of His power to do so, and accordingly to have designed to force Him to make such a display of His superhuman powers as would have induced all the Jews — and, indeed, the Romans too — to acknowledge Him King. (de Cordova: 542)

In 1902, Elgar faced a massive task: 'I am now plotting GIGANTIC WORX', he told Ivor Atkins that July (Moore 1984a: 372). *The Apostles* was originally intended to be the first part of a trilogy, a musical study of Christianity the size and nature of which reflects the inspiration of Wagner's *Ring*. Though Elgar had probably been contemplating a sacred equivalent of the *Ring* for some time, his ideas may have been consolidated when in 1902 he visited Bayreuth again (his last visit to the Wagner Festival) and heard the first three operas of the *Ring* as well as *Parsifal* and *Der fliegende Holländer*. (Making Mary Magdalene, not an apostle, one of *The Apostles*'s chief characters, may have been suggested by *Parsifal*'s Kundry.) The project was Elgar's most ambitious ever.

Ultimately, Elgar's growing disillusionment prevented him from seeing the oratorio cycle through: *The Apostles* and *The Kingdom* were to have been followed by a third part called *The Last Judgement*, *The Saints*, or *The Fulfilment*, but his plans were never accomplished. Indeed, when he reached the end of *The Kingdom*, he was still far from his original goal. The librettos of both completed works were assembled from the Bible by Elgar himself; Dora Penny recalled his study at the time as 'full of Bibles' (Powell: 39), and indeed his library included a large number of religious books. Many were collected with the practical aim of compiling librettos, but there is no doubting that Elgar's knowledge of theology and church history was impressive. (Some of his library is now at the Birthplace Museum; and Young 1955, pp. 254-5 lists many of his theological books.) *The Apostles*, comprising a Prologue and seven scenes, encompasses the calling of the disciples, the Beatitudes, Jesus's works on earth, his betrayal, passion, and ascension. *The Kingdom*, in five parts, picks up the story, describing Pentecost, and the establishment of the Apostles in Jerusalem.

Throughout the winter of 1902-3 Elgar worked feverishly at *The Apostles*. One source of inspiration was a photograph he acquired of the painting *The Temptation of Christ* by the Russian artist Ivan Kramskoy. Elgar described it as 'my ideal picture of the lonely Christ as I have *tried* (and tried hard) to realise' (Moore 1984a: 401). The artist himself summed it up as follows: 'This is no Christ, it is the image of the sorrows of humanity which are known to all of us' (Hamilton: 264). (Elgar's copy of the picture now hangs in the Birthplace Museum.) As Elgar had done when composing *Gerontius*, he wrote to Hubert Leicester asking for some music from St George's, which he acknowledged with the comment, 'I may use the old tone for the *Meeting* of the Apostles'. Though plainsong (notably the Gregorian antiphon 'O sacrum convivium,' and the gradual 'Constitues eos') and Hebrew chant (the latter, drawn from Pauer's collection of *Traditional Hebrew Melodies* on the suggestion of Rabbi Frances Cohen, was used to depict dawn in Jerusalem) was incorporated, nothing of Elgar's own church music appears to have found its way into the oratorio. He completed *The Apostles* with only months to spare: there had been interruptions and conducting engagements, including the first London performance of *The Dream of Gerontius* in the unconsecrated Westminster Cathedral. At last Elgar was rewarded with a widely acclaimed premiere, when he conducted *The Apostles* at Birmingham on 14 October 1903.

Elgar's use of Gregorian tunes in both *The Apostles* and *Gerontius* is interesting in the light of Pope Pius X's famous *Moto Proprio* issued in November 1903, a document which sought to reform church music and restore Gregorian chant to wide use. Evidently, plainchant had been part of the musical fabric at St George's, Worcester, for many years, but Elgar favoured continuing the use of Viennese Masses, too. His view on the *Moto Proprio* was recorded by Philip Leicester in 1910: 'Said Church had never interfered with architecture but had left it to suit the needs of each country & time. Had told Perosi he did not know the world (or something to that effect) & that national tastes in musical matters differed'. On his visit to Rome in 1907, Elgar had met Dom Lorenzo Perosi, the organist of the Sistine Chapel, and a composer himself, who had been put in charge of effecting these reforms.

Six weeks after the *Apostles* premiere the family embarked for Italy, where at Alassio Elgar found inspiration for his concert overture *In the South*, repeating the pattern of two years earlier when he followed a big choral work, *Gerontius*, with a concert overture, *Cockaigne*. After Christmas he became restless, and foul weather provided an excuse to return to England. There a busy schedule awaited him, including a three-day festival of his music at Covent Garden in March, which included the premiere of *In the South*. The first two nights were attended by the King and Queen, an indication of Elgar's stature as a national composer. In the ensuing months, many honours followed: election to the Atheneum and an honorary doctorate of music from Durham were a prelude to being knighted at Buckingham Palace on 5 July. Within the space of a few years Elgar had progressed from being a provincial composer struggling against prejudices of class and religion, to being the most celebrated national composer, accepted by the Establishment. Soon the first biography of him, by Robert Buckley, was published.

Appropriately, the next move was to a larger house, Plas Gwyn on the outskirts of Hereford, at the beginning of July 1904. Work continued as usual, with the sketching of *The Kingdom*. But composition, interrupted by chores such as proof-checking for Novello, was slow, and the remainder of the year saw only the third *Pomp and Circumstance* March completed. That winter he turned his attention to writing the *Introduction and Allegro* for the strings of the newly-founded London Symphony Orchestra. It is both majestic and haunting: Alice Elgar summed it up when she told Jaeger 'Many people think it is the finest thing he has written'. Although the *Introduction and Allegro* had been committed to paper within the space of a few weeks, one of its themes had been with Elgar since his Welsh holiday in 1901. He labelled it 'Ynys

Lochtyn', but as he recalled in a programme note: 'The sketch was forgotten until a short time ago, when it was brought to mind by hearing, far down our Valley of the Wye, a song similar to those so pleasantly heard on Ynys Lochten...the work is really a tribute to that sweet borderland where I have made my home' (Moore 1984a: 451-2). Throughout his life Elgar derived inspiration from the countryside, especially that of Worcestershire and the Malvern Hills, Herefordshire and the Welsh borderlands. A small number of works carry special associations with individual places. On the *Gerontius* manuscript he wrote 'the trees are singing my music — or have I sung theirs?'. Setting the passage 'the rushing of the...summer wind among the lofty pines' brought to mind the great trees at his old Spetchley Park school. In *Caractacus*, the little 'Woodland Interlude' evokes 'the forest near the Severn — Morning', and the depiction of Swallow's Gloucestershire orchard in *Falstaff* is a gentle English idyll. Elgar's fondness for the Worcester riverside found voice in the *Severn Suite*. But it is all too easy to read back into his music images of the landscape in what is now known as 'Elgar country'. Elgar felt deeply about his native countryside, yet he visited places, often on his long cycle rides, to find inspiration rather than to transcribe the scene directly. The outdoors fired his imagination, but there is seldom anything in the musical notes themselves that can be identified with it. Although Elgar's music is widely perceived as English, does it really *sound* English? The roots of Elgar's individual musical idiom are all continental: Haydn and Mozart early on, later a mixture of Schumann, Brahms, Wagner, and Dvořák, leavened by the lighter French music of Saint-Saëns, Chabrier, and Delibes. Significantly, he paid little attention to the English folk music that was being collected during his lifetime.

A major interruption of his creative work was his appointment as the first Peyton Professor of Music at the University of Birmingham. Elgar accepted the post only after much indecision — his early associations with Birmingham, and the fact that the endowment for the Chair of Music was offered on condition that Elgar should be the first professor, weighed heavily on him — but with an escape clause that he could resign after three years if he wished. This he did. When Granville Bantock succeeded him in 1908, Peyton wrote to the university secretary: 'I am pleased to think that there will be now a prospect of some satisfactory results attending the existence of a musical professorship in the university...The actual result & virtual waste of time, has, I need not say, been a great disappointment to me' (Kennedy: 178). Unsatisfactory though the post may have been for both parties, that paints a negative picture of the extraordinary series of lectures which Elgar delivered, all of which attracted great interest, both from the press and leading musicians of the day. If the ordeal caused Elgar much anxiety, his wide-ranging lectures touched many a raw nerve. He revealed a vision for an English school of composition, even for a National Opera, but most of his views, whether so intended or not, were interpreted as thinly veiled attacks on the musical establishment. Elgar's comments widened the already existing gulf between him and Stanford, and by extension most of the London music college fraternity, though his relations with Hubert Parry were always to remain an exception. Perhaps it was their common border country background (Parry's attachment to Gloucestershire was as deep as Elgar's to Worcestershire), but there was a mutual understanding between the two, as reflected in Parry's oration on the occasion of Elgar's honorary doctorate from Oxford in 1905.

By now awards were being virtually heaped on Elgar, with honorary degrees soon to follow from Aberdeen, Pennsylvania, and Birmingham. The one he perhaps valued most was that from Yale in June 1905, which had come at the invitation of Professor S.S. Sanford, dedicatee of the *Introduction and Allegro*. It was the Elgars' first visit to the United States. They sailed home from New York in time for the Three Choirs Festival, at Worcester that year. For Elgar the highlight of the festival was being made an Honorary Freeman of the City, an accolade conferred on him by the new Mayor, his friend since the St George's days, Hubert Leicester. Following the ceremony at the Guildhall, the company set off for the Cathedral for a performance of *Gerontius*, passing under a window where Elgar's old father, too ill to have attended the ceremony, watched the procession. Ivor Atkins's *Hymn of Faith*, set to a text compiled from the Bible by Elgar, was also included in the festival that year. At the end of the festival he set off for a fortnight on a cruise of the Mediterranean, taking in such places as Athens, Constantinople, and Smyrna. The delicate, evocative writing in his piano piece *In Smyrna* records his impressions.

Another civic honour, the Mayorship of Hereford, was offered round about this time. Elgar, ever sensitive to religious prejudice, sought the advice of Hubert Leicester, himself Mayor of Worcester.

> A deputation came to-day from the Corporation inviting me to be Mayor of Hereford. It would, of course, in my case be more or less an honorary appointment but I should have much to do: *all* seems clear except the question of Church.
>
> Did you attend the Cathedral? i.e. in state — I don't see why I should not if we go to the Festival services, but I would like to have ten minutes to talk with you as I pass there tomorrow...

In the event he turned the Mayorship down, writing to Leicester his reasons for declining:

> I refused to take this Office: I found that some of the folk did not know we are Catholics & I found privately that those who did know fully expected me to go to the Cathedral: to save discussion I made no terms but simply refused 'on many grounds'. (Letter dated 3 November 1905. BL Add MS 60357, ff. 84-85)

The death of Elgar's father at the end of April 1906 while the composer was preparing to conduct *Gerontius* and *The Apostles* at the Cincinnati May Festival came as a blow to him, and upon his return Elgar struggled to get back into the composition of *The Kingdom*, promised for the Birmingham Festival that October. When music flowed again he wrote to Jaeger: 'the whole thing is intentionally less mystic than the A.: the *men* are alive & working & the atmosphere is meant to be more direct & simple' (Kennedy: 202). Indeed, both oratorios after *Gerontius* are more restrained. Vaughan Williams suggested to Michael Kennedy (Kennedy: 206) that in *The Apostles* Elgar was 'oppressed by the fact that he was writing for the Church of England'; if anything, this might have been truer of *The Kingdom*. But Elgar's letter to Jaeger of 1908 explaining that he could not complete the trilogy — 'I am not allowed to beg a dispensation of a benevolent providence who objects to the world being saved or purified or improved by a mere musician' (Young 1965: 275) — suggests that his aims were widely ecumenical anyway. Certainly, both *The Apostles* and *The Kingdom* took a safe, non-sectarian view of early Christianity. As with both *The Apostles* and *Gerontius*, Elgar dedicated *The Kingdom* 'A.M.D.G.'. There is no doubt that Elgar was deeply affected by the piece; he was seen at the premiere by members of the chorus to be weeping while conducting. Was he shedding tears for his own faltering faith? Did his instincts tell him that the trilogy would remain unfinished? His somewhat cynical, detached mood is revealed in a letter he wrote to Ivor Atkins just before Christmas that year:

> Times is awry...I know that, owing to the ripeness of the year that Xtians wax gross in their food & religion, of whilk twain the first concerns you not whilst the second may hold you fast to tinkle silver into collecting plates with warily selected tunes — such is the Xtian way. (Moore 1984a: 506)

In public he had been putting on a brave face. At an Oxford University Extension Lecture on Renaissance Art in January 1906 he remarked that the relationship between art and religion was absolute, and according to the *Hereford Times*, 'said that it always struck him very forcibly that the whole basis of art was religion'(Young 1986: 8). But in private it would seem that the conflicting demands of Catholic optimism and romantic disillusionment were confusing him, and his outlook became increasingly humanistic. He attended church less and less. (During the Hereford years, when he went to church, it was usually to Canon Dolman's church in Hereford, St Francis Xavier, or to Bullingham, Rotherwas, and Belmont Abbey [Hodgkins: 15].) After *The Kingdom* he wrote no more large-scale religious works, the only sacred music being small pieces for special occasions. After he gave up the oratorio trilogy a stream of major symphonic works followed, though it was two years before the first of them appeared.

January and February 1907 found the Elgars in Italy again, and in March the composer set off on yet another American visit, to conduct *The Apostles* and *The Kingdom* in New York (where he declined a request to lead a meeting to pray for the failure of

Strauss's *Salome*), and the 'Enigma' Variations in Chicago and Pittsburgh. He returned in April, ready to face another milestone in his life. The following month he told Jaeger: 'I shall be fifty next week so they tell me, but I don't know it. I have my pipe & the bicycle & heavenly country to ride in — so an end. I take no interest whatever in music now & just "edit" a few old boyish M.S.S.' (Young 1965: 269); and in June he wrote: '...I am doing trifles: poor things but mine own boyish thoughts' (Young 1965: 269). Elgar was going though old manuscripts, working on the final revision of his early music into *The Wand of Youth* Suite No. 1.

Among these 'trifles' were psalm chants that were included in the 'New Cathedral Psalter' when it appeared in 1909. He produced two single chants for the Venite (Appendix One: 2.5), one in G major and one in D major; and two double chants in D major, for Psalms 68 and 75 (Appendix One: 2.6). The chants were composed in the spring of 1907, but submitted to Novello only on 1 April 1909, as a note under the sketches for the double chants (Source A) indicates.

Although made up of the simplest musical material, they bear definite fingerprints of the composer. The single chant in D major resembles a passage in the elegy *They are at Rest* (1909), which in turn was later echoed in *The Spirit of England*. In tonality and melodic outline the double chant for Psalm 68 is reminiscent of a passage in the Violin Concerto (1910), which itself resembles a motive in the second movement of the Symphony No. 2 (1911). All these passages are dominated by the Elgarian falling 4th.

Example 17 (a) Chant for Psalm 68, bars 8-10:

Example 17 (b) Violin Concerto, first movement, bars 1-2:

Example 17 (c) Second Symphony, second movement, bars 19-20:

Sketches for two chants that were not published (Appendix One: 2.7) also survive. They were probably written at the same time, but both the single chant in A minor and the double chant in C minor are clumsy, and were probably abandoned by the composer.

Another manuscript has the four published chants written out together in Elgar's hand (Appendix One: 2.5, Source B; Appendix One: 2.6, Source B), with an Elgarian doodle on the reverse (BL Add MS 69827: f. 36v.). It consists of two single and two double chants, forty-three bars in all, arranged in a continuous sequence, beginning with a key signature of seven flats and returning there in a bar marked *dal segno*. Elgar's heading sums it up: 'Chant sequence form (I think) invented by E.E.?'.

Elgar's fiftieth birthday brought renewed energy in his work, and found him sketching a symphony, a violin concerto, even a string quartet — a form he had not tackled since his youth. With his reputation established through 'acceptable' works, he now hoped to enjoy the indulgence of writing what he wanted. A string quartet did not materialise for another decade, but much of the music from the one he began in 1907 was incorporated into the First Symphony. Composition was delayed by an unproductive winter break in Italy (virtually all he had to show for it was the part song *A Christmas Greeting*, written to Alice's words, for the choristers of Hereford Cathedral). Shortly after arriving in Rome he had written to Frank Schuster: 'Here is my Mecca & I love it *all* — Note the fact that I am pagan not Xtian at present' (Moore 1984a: 520). Disillusion is evident in the following conversation with Hubert Leicester, noted down by Leicester's son Philip on 17 June 1908:

> If you have any religious feeling whatever, don't go to Rome — everything money — clergy gorgeous & grasping...'Special music' (bombardon & side drum & Gounod's 'Ave Maria'). Present Pope a good holy simple man but knows nothing...should be replaced by a permanent Commission with secretary who could be dismissed.

EDWARD ELGAR: SACRED MUSIC

Elgar's disenchantment with conventional religion was growing stronger, and with it came a gradual withdrawal from formal modes of worship, but he always maintained an interest in church affairs and continued to support his old church with donations. His correspondence with Hubert Leicester reveals that for much of his life Elgar received regularly copies of the *Tablet* from Leicester.

Around this time there were thoughts of Elgar's providing further music for the Anglican liturgy. In 1908 he received a suggestion from Novello about setting a whole Communion Service. Most English composers had made such settings for the Anglican Church, and the publishers evidently thought that one from a composer of Elgar's stature would be a welcome addition to the repertory. Although Elgar had composed movements for the Roman Catholic Mass in his St George's days, and would undoubtedly have encountered Anglican communion settings, he replied rather vaguely to Alfred Littleton of Novello on 1 June 1908:

> I don't quite know what a *full* Communion Service includes. I shall be very pleased to try my hand: will you send me two complete services containing the whole of the things necessary to be set — very simple things will do[,] preferably by authors I hold in awe and reverence, Wesley to wit. (Moore 1987: 695)

The letter shows an odd, possibly affected, ignorance of Church of England rite. There is no evidence in any of the surviving sketchbooks that Elgar even began to sketch anything.

The year drew to a close with a triumph for Elgar, the premiere of his First Symphony under the baton of Hans Richter, its dedicatee, in Manchester on 3 December 1908. English music had come of age and produced a work worthy to be put alongside masterpieces of the repertory. Within a year the symphony was heard in numerous performances, as far afield as St Petersburg, New York, and Sydney. Elgar's (German-derived) technique had assumed socio-political importance: he was able to rival even Richard Strauss, and to write orchestral music unhindered by the lack of an English symphonic tradition. Yet, although Elgar had won the success he craved so much, he ended 1908 in his all-too-characteristic self-pitying mode. He wrote to his friend Adela Schuster:

> I receive heaps of letters from persons known and unknown telling me how it uplifts them: I wish it uplifted me — I have just paid rent, Land Tax, Income Tax & a variety of other things due today and there are children yapping at the door. 'Christians awake! Salute the "yappy" morn'. I saluted it about seven o'clock, quite dark, made a fire in the Ark [his chemistry laboratory at the bottom of the garden] & mused on the future of a bad cold in my head. (Moore 1984a: 548)

Another visit to Italy, in 1909, was overshadowed by news of Jaeger's death on 18 May. Elgar, Alice and Carice had gone in April 1909 to stay with an American friend, Mrs Julia Worthington, at her villa in Careggi, near Florence. Before long Alice Elgar wrote to Alice Stuart-Wortley: 'The air is perfect & it is all beautiful, and *beautiful* new tunes have been written' (Moore 1989: 29). Elgar began a sketch-book labelled 'Opera in three acts' (BL Add MS 63161), but this came to nothing, and he also failed to make much progress with the Violin Concerto. However, he was able to complete the imposing part-song *Go, Song of Mine* and also planned a suite of them. In the sketch-book from 1909 (BL Add MS 63161) he listed: 'Choral Suite — I Intro., II In a Vineyard, III Angelus, IV Dance, V Vintage, VI Envoi'. *Angelus* (Appendix One: 2.8) was the only movement completed, and it became Op. 56 No.1. It is possible that Elgar felt himself unable to complete the suite because of his sadness at Jaeger's death, but he had already finished the *Angelus* before that event, as his letter to Clayton of Novello dated 13 May indicates:

> I enclose a short pt song — one, I hope of a series — will you have it set up in 8 vo. the usual way for me to see a proof as soon as possible[?] (Moore 1987: 722)

Other music from the sketches was later incorporated into *The Crown of India* Suite.

Though not strictly a church work, the religious sentiments of the *Angelus* (the text attributed 'from the Tuscan dialect' — a clue to Elgar's authorship) would have appealed to the composer who sought solace in memories of his youth. *Angelus* is also an effective

Tuscan evocation, and the sojourn in Careggi had obviously inspired Elgar: not only had he planned the series of part-songs depicting various scenes, but he also contemplated a *Tuscan Fantastico* (BL Add MS 63157).

During these years much of Elgar's music — notably the Violin Concerto and Second Symphony — was associated with Alice Stuart-Wortley, and even this small piece reflects the intense, albeit subdued, passion which characterizes the music linked with her. (She was the daughter of the Pre-Raphaelite painter Millais, and a few years earlier had given Elgar an engraving of her father's portrait of Cardinal Newman.) Elgar commented on the words when he wrote to her, offering to dedicate it:

> ...they are of the place & not far from your own monastery on the Fiesole road of which C.B.S.W. [Charles Stuart-Wortley] has memories also[.] Anyway it would give me the greatest pleasure to put your beloved name on it if you both allow it. (Moore 1989: 30)

In the same letter, dated 23 June 1909, Elgar enclosed a proof of the music and asked for advice on the wording of the dedication:

> I wanted to *bring*...the enclosed little remembrance of Careggi...had no time, alas! & ask if your name may go on it: please look at the title carefully & tell me if I have it right & tell me how to amend it or to remove it altogether — it looks so *gastfully* formal.
> ...Please return these rough proofs to me & I will follow your commands. (Moore 1989: 29-3)

Alice Stuart-Wortley accepted the dedication and Elgar acknowledged this in a letter of 29 June:

> In awful haste [—] I send one word of thanks for your letter accepting my little dedication: it is so sweet of you & your amended version of the formula is so much better than my *modest* & muddy brain could have attained to. I was afraid the simple words might be too papistical for you — or for your family! (Moore 1989: 30)

The *Angelus* is a small, beautifully written gem. Its form is simple, each of the two verses consists of balanced halves. The imitation of Angelus bells is skillfully achieved through interlocking alto and tenor ostinatos, set to the words 'Ave, Mary!':

Example 18: 'Angelus', bars 7-12:

Another church work, *They are at Rest* (Appendix One: 2.9), followed that year. It was written at the request of the Master of the King's Musick, Sir Walter Parratt (Parratt, who died in 1924, was succeeded as Master of the King's Musick by Elgar), for music to be sung at the Royal Mausoleum at Frogmore, Windsor Home Park, on the tenth anniversary of Queen Victoria's death. It was performed there on 22 January 1910.

The elegy was composed at Plas Gwyn, Hereford, in November 1909, after a long series of concerts. Elgar turned to Cardinal Newman for the text, a poem dealing with similar subject matter to *The Dream of Gerontius*. It was the only other musical use that Elgar ever made of Newman's writings. Queen Victoria was of a low-church inclination; her views on a commemorative ode by two of England's most distinguished Catholics might have been amusing.

The beginning of *They are at Rest* echoes the openings of two other contemporary works by Elgar, the Violin Concerto and 'Go, Song of Mine'. All three pieces share the same tonal orientation, and it is as if the figure became increasingly condensed:

Example 19 (a): 'Go, Song of Mine', bars 1-6:

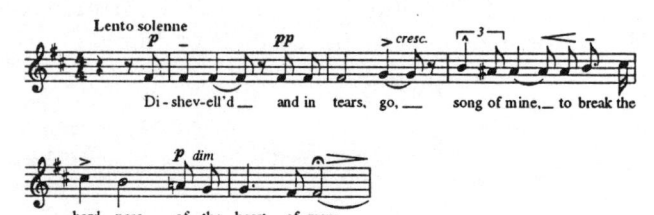

[musical notation: Lento solenne, with text "Di-shev-ell'd and in tears, go, song of mine, to break the hard-ness of the heart of man:"]

Example 19 (b): Violin Concerto, first movement, bars 1-2:

[musical notation, mf]

Example 19 (c): 'They are at rest', bars 1-2:

[musical notation: Lento e sostenuto, with text "They are at rest"]

Although the music was intended for a ceremonial occasion, its elegiac character sets it far apart from most of Elgar's occasional music. It is stark, simple, and consists of just two verses, scored for unaccompanied SATB. Elgar appears to have deliberately withheld much colour from the elegy, though it features some subtle word-painting. The reference to Eden and the river would have evoked memories of his childhood and the River Severn of which he was so fond:

> They are at rest;
> We may not stir the heav'n of their repose
> By rude invoking voice, or prayer addrest
> In waywardness to those
> Who in the mountain grots of Eden lie,
> And hear the fourfold river as it murmurs by.

3. 1910-1934

At the close of the Edwardian era Elgar's popularity was at its height, and his creative powers were at their peak. Though a violin concerto had long been on his mind (indeed, he had sketched and destroyed one back in 1890) it was in a concentrated spurt between January and July 1910 that most of the Violin Concerto in B minor came into being. Elgar dedicated it to the great violinist Fritz Kreisler, the soloist at the premiere on 10 November, but an enigmatic quotation in Spanish at the head of the score, 'Aqui està encerrada el alma de...' ('Herein is enshrined the soul of...'), reveals the deeply personal nature of the music.

The inscription on the frontispiece of the Second Symphony, 'Dedicated to the Memory of His late Majesty, King Edward VII', records the King's death in May 1910. Yet the dedication obscured its wider meaning, which Alice Elgar hinted at in her diary: 'it résumés our human life, delight, regrets, farewell, the saddest mood & then the strong man's triumph'. Certainly, the symphony's elegiac and at times apocalyptic vein has less to do with Edward VII's death than with the stormclouds which even then were gathering over Europe. Though the war was still four years away, the aspirations and interests of European countries were already colliding. Elgar, who thought that there was 'music in the air, music all around' and that composition involved 'taking as much as you require' must have been appalled by what he sensed around him. The massive brutality of which the symphony's third movement (Rondo) speaks suggests that Elgar had glimpsed the impending horror before the politicians sensed it. This music is the most 'demonic' he ever wrote (certainly more so than the Demons' Chorus in *Gerontius*) and seems to represent a direction from which Elgar, probably consciously, turned back. He trod very few new paths thereafter. Indeed some works, like *The Music Makers* (1912) for instance, were to be deliberately retrogressive.

Only days after conducting the symphony's premiere in May 1911, Elgar was awarded his highest honour, the Order of Merit. But at the same time the tide of opinion appeared to be turning, his fortunes seemed to be waning. Audiences failed to recognize the message of the symphony or the combination of Elgar's private and public faces which exists side by side in the work, and the premiere was no more than politely received. The music (its scherzo, particularly) speaks of tension and war; perhaps the mood of the work did not match the confidence of the public, which was eagerly awaiting the Coronation that summer.

Naturally, Elgar had his part to play in that celebration. *O Hearken Thou* (Appendix One: 3.1) was composed at the request of Frederick Bridge, organist of Westminster Abbey, to be sung as an Offertorium during King George V's Coronation on 22 June 1911; Elgar also wrote his *Coronation March* for the occasion. He was unhappy about writing the work, and Rosa Burley recalled that he was dissatisfied with the circumstances, 'either because he was asked to contribute only an offertorium and a Coronation March or because the fee offered was inadequate' (Burley and Carruthers: 189). To add to Elgar's tribulations, the work was written shortly before his departure, late in March 1911, for a tour of Canada and the United States which he was to describe as a 'worse than nightmare' experience (Kennedy: 237). A bad cold had forced the postponement of his sailing for Canada; during his convalescence Elgar was able to complete the Offertorium. He wrote to Alfred Littleton of Novello on 16 March:

> I have an awful cold & chill — I may be able to go to Canada as the horrid thing is at present only in my head — there's plenty of room there you'll say! I am not allowed out.
> — This only to say I have finished the Offertory for Sir F. Bridge & have sent the voc.sc. arrgt & full score to him by to-night's post. (Moore 1987: 739)

O Hearken Thou was evidently well received although Elgar was not present. By the time he received the news that he was to have the Order of Merit conferred on him, he had already declared his intention not to attend the Coronation. The Preface to 'The Form and Order of Their Majesties' Coronation' had the following to say:

> The setting written specially for this occasion by Sir Edward Elgar is in every way a worthy example of English music, exhibiting in every line that spiritual intensity so characteristic of the composer. Amongst many striking progressions, the final cadence will be particularly noted, while the impression given by the work is exactly what it should be — a reverent supplication.

The work is subdued for a Coronation, and the *Coronation March*, intended as the Recessional in the Coronation service, is also dark in colour. Together these works seem to suggest Elgar's premonition of what the new reign would have in store.

Formally the piece is straightforward. It reflects the other work that was occupying his mind at the time: while he was at work on *O Hearken Thou* the proofs of the Second Symphony were still being read. There are echoes of the plunging figure of the opening of the symphony in a phrase from the Offertorium:

Example 20 (a): Second Symphony, first movement, bar 3:

Example 20 (b): 'O Hearken Thou', bars 20-23:

The Offertorium is a setting of Psalm 5, verse 2. Eventually Elgar produced three versions of the piece: besides the original Offertorium there is a version with a Latin text ('Intende vocis orationis meae'), also published by Novello, and one in English which incorporates verse 3 of the Psalm — though the setting of the extra words betrays the fact that they are adapted to already existing music.

EDWARD ELGAR: SACRED MUSIC

Though Alice Elgar's mission in life, nurturing her husband's genius, was selfless and unstinting (to the extent that she would even rule out bars on his manuscript paper), she was also driven by social ambition, perhaps a desire to prove her disapproving relatives' condemnation of their marriage unfounded. That ambition required them to be part of London's social and art circle, and in 1912 she achieved her aim of moving to the capital. At Severn House, as they named their splendid Norman Shaw home in Hampstead, the visitors included such people as Shalyapin, Paderewski, Siegfried Wagner, Yeats, and Henry James.

Elgar's involvement in London's musical life increased, with his becoming Principal Conductor of the London Symphony Orchestra, in succession to Hans Richter, for the 1911-12 season. Another project was the masque *The Crown of India*, which opened at the London Coliseum on 11 March 1912, to celebrate the Coronation of the new King and Queen as Emperor and Empress of India. Elgar conducted the run, during which time he wrote to his friend Frances Colvin:

> When I write a big serious work e.g. Geronitus we have to starve & go without fires for twelve months as a reward: this small effort allows me to buy scientific works I have yearned for & spend my time between the Coliseum & the old bookshops... Ha! ha! I found a lovely old volume 'Tracts against *Popery*' — I appeased Alice by saying I bought it to prevent other people seeing it — but it wd make a cat laugh. (Moore 1984a: 630)

During the run, a variety of other pieces occupied his mind. He put the finishing touches to the anthem *Great is the Lord* (Appendix One: 3.2) which he had begun writing in 1910. Work on the anthem had begun in the wake of the Violin Concerto, in August 1910. Elgar turned to it as relief from the concerto orchestration and checking of proofs, completing most of the compostion in 1910. But it was put aside until March 1912, when he polished it up. Elgar wrote to Henry Clayton of Novello on 29 March:

> I am sending a gigantic Anthem to the firm which I fear will be commercially not much to you — the organ part is important & must be on three staves; it is very big stuff of Wesley

length but alas! not of Wesley grandeur. (Moore 1987: 765-6)

By the summer, Elgar was occupied with *The Music Makers*, but his thoughts returned to the anthem. On 3 June, the day after his fifty-fifth birthday, he went to the Temple Church to hear Walford Davies play it over (Moore 1984a: 635).

One of the first people to receive a copy was Ivor Atkins, who acknowledged it in a letter of 7 July 1912:

> Thank you immensely for the copy of the anthem. It *is* gorgeous. I played it over to my [choir]boys and they loved it and their keenness was good to see.
>
> I made a sort of running transcription of it as I went along (with fine effect!) and it sounded great. When the Kings were assembled they really *were* amazed *and* dismayed. I'm longing to hear it done — we shall do it early next term (there is no time to get it up before the end of term).
>
> It really is splendid music and some of the middle section fairly blazes, the pedal part cunning to a degree...
>
> The simple greatness of the end is you all over.
>
> Where do you get these haunting phrases from? (Atkins: 239-240)

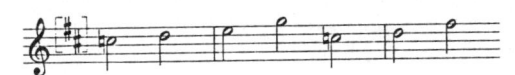

The first performance was conducted by Sir Frederick Bridge at a special service to mark the 250th anniversary of the Royal Society, held on 16 July 1912 in Westminster Abbey. The anthem was dedicated to the Dean of Wells, the Very Reverend J. Armitage Robinson, whom Elgar first met by chance while walking in the hills above Alassio (where he wrote his overture *In the South*) in Italy in 1904, and who had helped the composer with suggestions for the Kingdom libretto.

The grand scale of the organ accompaniment lent itself to orchestration, a task which Elgar undertook in February 1913, judging by the date in the manuscript (Source C), but which he may not have finished completely for some months. He wrote to Clayton of

Novello on 7 July:

> I think there wd be no difficulty in letting you have the score of the Anthem by the second week of Sept or even a week earlier so that ought to satisfy Mr. Crowe. (Moore 1987: 771)

On 8 February 1914 Elgar referred to the orchestration in a letter to Clayton:

> I hope Atkins may do the Psalm [48 at the 1914 Worcester Festival]. By the way was it ever done at Chichester (?)— I forget the place proposed but I scored it for you last year: were the parts used? I am writing to Atkins & will tell him it is scored. (Moore 1987: 778)

This he did the next day:

> What about that PsXLVIII? — I scored it last year, but if not possible for orch cd it be done at one of the services with organ? (Atkins: 253)

In other letters Elgar urged Atkins to perform his new setting of Psalm 29 (see p.97), though in the end it was *Great is the Lord* that was sung by the combined choirs of Worcester, Hereford, and Gloucester cathedrals, with organ accompaniment, in the closing service of the Festival on Friday 11 September 1914.

Although the early sketches (Source A) are vague and consist mainly of the melody and bass line, Elgar seems to have had the dignified opening in mind right from beginning the composition. The anthem is in D, the relative major of the B minor Violin Concerto, and not surprisingly, some motives are similar. The opening figure of the anthem bears a close resemblance to the primary subject of the first movement of the concerto:

Example 21 (a): 'Great is the Lord', bars 2-3:

Example 21 (b): Violin Concerto, first movement, bars 1-2:

A figure in the final section, too, imitates the concerto's finale:

Example 22 (a): 'Great is the Lord', bars 172-174:

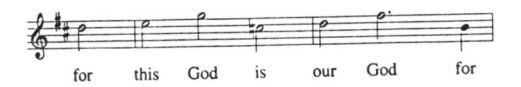

for this God is our God for

Example 22 (b): Violin Concerto, third movement, bars 32-33:

In scope, *Great is the Lord* resembles an episode from one of Elgar's oratorios. It is constructed on a grand scale, as the dramatic possibilities of Psalm 48 are exploited. The text was constructed by the composer, using the Prayer Book as well as the Authorised and Revised Versions of the Bible.

Since the text suggests no distinct form, the setting is sectional (though the beginning and end of the anthem are related motivically). Elgar's response to the text is straightforward, reflecting the dramatic moods of the Psalm (bustling rhythms for 'For lo! the kings assembled themselves'; gentle dance-like movement at 'Let mount Zion be glad, let the daughters of Judah rejoice'). The calm centre of the piece is a bass solo in A flat major, a startling contrast from the tonic D major. This tritone juxtaposition echoes the A flat-D minor contrast in the opening movement of the First Symphony (1907-8). Perhaps the change of key serves to reinforce the lyricism of the middle section, which contrasts in nearly every way with the rest of the piece, where imposing moments reflect Elgar's mastery of ceremonial music.

Around this time, Elgar received a suggestion from the Duke of Argyll for an opera about St Columba. One disadvantage from an operatic point of view was the saint's dislike of women: 'he wd.

allow nothing of female sex — not even a cow — in Iona' (Anderson: 106). Instead, after completing the anthem, Elgar turned his thoughts to *The Music Makers*, a commission for the Birmingham Festival late in 1912. A secular choral cantata on an Arthur O'Shaughnessy poem, it is one of the composer's most backward-looking pieces. In some ways, especially in its self-indulgence, it is comparable to Strauss's *Ein Heldenleben;* there are quotations from Elgar's earlier works. The poem deals with the loneliness of the artist, and writing the work left Elgar in a deep depression that lasted for several months. In March 1913, contemplating his next commission, the symphonic poem *Falstaff*, he wrote a letter to the dedicatee of *The Music Makers*, Nicholas Kilburn, which reflects his spiritual outlook at the time:

> Well, you talk mystically as becomes you & your northern atmosphere. I cannot follow you. I could have done a few years back — but the whole thing (no matter how one fights & avoids it) is merely commercial — this is forced into every fibre of me at every moment. Not long ago one could occasionally shake this off & forget, but an all-foolish providence takes care that it shall not be *un*remembered for a moment or so — & so?? You say 'we must look up'? To what? To whom? Why? 'The mind bold and independent, the purpose free must not think, must not hope' — Yet it seems sad that the only quotation I can find to fit my life comes from the Demons' chorus! a *fanciful* summing up!! (Letter dated 26 March 1913. (Moore 1984a: 643)

Elgar seemed to be avoiding composition. February had seen another trip to Italy, and March a week's break in Wales. Of that he wrote to Hubert Leicester, recounting how he had heard one of his early *O Salutaris* settings in a service at the church in Llandrindod Wells: 'the air is full of the old days to me — this morning the Harmonium played, by way of voluntary, the first *O Salutaris* I wrote — it came back like a shock as I had just been looking at its contemporaneous "Shed"'(BL Add MS 60357: ff. 128-129). In London he went to church hardly at all; Alice and Carice attended, usually St James's, Spanish Place, the Brompton Oratory, or the Hampstead church.

The Three Choirs Festival was scheduled for Worcester in 1914, and Ivor Atkins tried to persuade Elgar to complete the *Apostles* trilogy. He refused. His declining faith was soon to show itself in the complete absence of sacred music from his output, but 1914 brought two church pieces, the last he wrote for the church for fourteen years. His first work of the year was the anthem *Give unto the Lord*, a setting of Psalm 29 (Appendix One: 3.3); according to Lady Elgar's diary of 6 March 1914, he was '... much inclined to play with anything to avoid working at [the] Anthem' (Moore 1974: 7).

In scale, *Give unto the Lord* matches Elgar's other big anthem of the pre-war years, *Great is the Lord*. It is dedicated to George Martin, the organist of St Paul's Cathedral, who requested it for the Sons of the Clergy Festival held in the Cathedral in 1914. Elgar began work on the music on 20 January 1914; his orchestration was completed as late as April, but by 4 March Elgar had dispatched a vocal score to the publishers (Moore 1987: 783). The service took place on 30 April.

Elgar sent a copy of the work to Ivor Atkins on 15 April: 'Here is the new Anthem — it wd do well for your Sunday with full orch — thunderstorms & drums' (Atkins: 256). He was referring to the opening service of the Worcester Festival, which eventually took place without his work, and he had to be content with the performance in St Paul's Cathedral. Elgar was offended by the omission of *Give unto the Lord* from the Festival, for he wrote the following to Atkins on 2 July 1914:

> I have been rushed to a great extent or I should have written at once to say I do not understand on what ground you have withdrawn the anthem at the opening service.
>
> I have been wondering if I am really wanted at all, but I hesitate to withdraw entirely from the festival although there is no inducement for me to come: you see Gerontius 'goes' without me & it wd be quite a safe draw with you — the evening concert I am not keen about. So do not announce anything conducted by me for the present & I will see. (Atkins: 262)

Although Elgar's disillusionment with music and the world in general was to become more pronounced after the death of his wife, this was an early indication of that self-pitying tendency.

Shortly before the death of Alice Elgar in 1920, he offered the piece to Atkins again in a letter dated 15 February:

> I hope you will find room for the enclosed anthem — with big orch: you will see the reference to *peace* at the end— about as far as we can go under the circumstances. (Atkins: 305)

This would suggest that he was offering *Give unto the Lord* to Atkins instead of a new composition for the Worcester Festival of 1920, but once again Atkins declined to include it.

Elgar's sketches for *Give unto the Lord* (Source A) are incomplete and in places quite fragmentary, though they contain all the main thematic material. One idea which appears not to have been used is in another sketch-book (Source B), begun in 1901. It is in B minor, the key of the middle section of the anthem, and is marked "ps xxix", but does not resemble any of the published material. The vocal score which Elgar sent to the publishers (Source C) underwent only very minor alterations.

Elgar's setting is imposing and well suited to such occasions as the festival first performance in St Paul's Cathedral. Moore has commented that 'the ripe sequences served the comfortable Anglican style for such things' (Moore 1984a: 663). The dignified mood and impressive scoring for organ and large orchestra call to mind episodes in the oratorios. Graphic orchestral effects are introduced, especially in such passages as 'the God of glory thundereth' and 'the Lord breaketh the cedars of Lebanon'. But Elgar does not rely solely on orchestral colouring: attention is given to the vocal textures, for instance the open fifths and octaves of the choral writing at the passage 'strippeth the forests bare'.

As with *Great is the Lord*, there is no distinct form: the music reflects the changing moods of the text in a series of unconnected episodes. However, the tonal structure is clear. The outer sections are based in E-flat major and the lyrical middle section is in B minor, the key that had dominated much of Elgar's thinking from the composition of the Violin Concerto onwards. Not surprisingly, there are melodic similarities:

Example 23 (a): 'Give unto the Lord', bars 79-80:

Example 23 (b): Violin Concerto, first movement, bars 66-67:

Furthermore, the link is sometimes rhythmic: the syncopated figures that characterised some of the music in the Violin Concerto became a feature in the succeeding years and are even to be found in *Give unto the Lord*. In both examples the bass line moves mainly by thirds:

Example 24 (a): 'Give unto the Lord', bars 50-51:

Example 24 (b): Violin Concerto, first movement, bars 64-67:

Although the setting displays many notable traits of the composer's style, some shortcomings are also apparent. This is particularly true of the three-fold repetition of the short two bar phrase 'the blessing of peace' (bars 130-135), a sequence which seems commonplace for a composer of Elgar's stature; stock gestures elsewhere suggest that his heart was not quite in it. The strong and direct ending, and especially the organ's final unison chord, is typical of Elgar's style in works of this nature. But the spirit of affirmation in the closing lines, 'The Lord shall give strength unto his people; the Lord shall give his people the blessing of peace', rings hollow.

In view of what the year had in store, it is ironic to reflect on the title and the text of Elgar's next anthem, *Fear Not, O land*, a setting of verses from the book of Joel (Appendix One: 3.4). It was written in the spring of 1914, one of several small pieces on which Elgar had been working in the first half of the year. Many of these works were commissioned, though there is no record of any request for the anthem. It would appear that Elgar attached little importance to it as it bears no opus number.

The surviving sketches are mostly vague, but all the main thematic material is evident. In April 1914 Elgar dispatched his anthem to the publishers, where the proofs were read by John E. West. Novello offered Elgar fifty guineas for the copyright, and Elgar wrote to West on 11 June:

> I recognise your hand on the proofs of the little anthem & I have adopted all, I think, of your suggestions.
> I am still vague about marking the organ part — two manuals scourge me a great deal. Is it necessary to put any indication at the opening — & please look at p.2 the query (last stave) and my answer — if 'la melodia marcato' is too Italian perhaps *marcato* wd. be enough — on p.3 I have put *Clar.* to shew the solo effect desired but perhaps this is unusual & if adopted should be followed by other indications such as Diap[ason]s. 3 bars after R[ight] H[and] E♭ — & what about *Sw & Gt?* — is it usual in these small anthems to mention these. & 'coupled' &c. I am only anxious to make the thing Serviceable. (Moore 1987: 783)

The published score shows that all the indications Elgar requested were incorporated in some form or other.

The simple and direct style of *Fear Not, O land* indicates that it was written specifically with choirs of limited ability in mind. As such, it was first published in the Novello Octavo Series for Church Choirs with the subtitle 'Harvest Anthem (SATB) for Parish Choirs'.

1910-1934

Elgar had not written church music specifically for amateur choirs since his early years. His recent anthems had been written on a large scale for special occasions. The anthem is in ternary form, with the outer sections based on the same material. They are bold in character, and contrast with the more lyrical middle section, typical of the 'lighter' Elgar. Again, there is some picturesque word-painting where vigorously expressed sentiment gives way to tenderness for 'the beasts of the field' and 'the pastures of the wilderness'.

The Elgar Birthplace archives reveal one other small church music project which Elgar undertook in 1914, a tune to Dorothy F. Gurney's hymn 'O Perfect Love', dated 22 June 1914 (Appendix One: 3.5). Elgar's correspondence shows that the hymn tune was probably written by his close friend Alice Stuart-Wortley for the wedding of her niece, and given the necessary revision and harmonization by Elgar (Moore 1989: 132). Her name appears at the top of the manuscript, but their collaboration is revealed in the letters from the composer to her written in July 1914 (Moore 1989: 132,134). In his last reference to it, dated July 16, Elgar wrote: 'I am glad that Hymn tune went well — I am sure no one could help loving it — perhaps not as much as I do' (Moore 1989: 134). An earlier letter (July 14) refers to 'your beautiful tune', which suggests it was Mrs Stuart-Wortley's work; certainly she was an accomplished musician who would easily have been capable of writing it, but it is worth bearing in mind that in letters to her Elgar referred to the Violin Concerto and Second Symphony as 'our own concerto' and 'your symphony'.

Early in 1914, Elgar took the momentous step of entering a recording studio, the initial move in what proved to be a long and fruitful association between him and the gramophone industry, indeed, one of the most significant partnerships of its kind. On 21 January he recorded his little orchestral piece *Carissima*, even before it had received its public premiere, and by the end of June he had signed a contract with The Gramophone Company. After Elgar's visit to the Leicesters on his birthday earlier that month, Philip Leicester noted that he 'seemed very satisfied with the prospect of mechanical royalties & surprised us with details of the huge traffic in gramophone & records. Altogether he takes a brighter view of the commercial side of his music than he did 2 or

3 years ago'. Given Elgar's lifelong curiosity for things mechanical, it was natural that he should take both a musical and a scientific interest in these new developments. He was one of the first composers to embrace the new technology wholeheartedly, and by the end of his life he had left as a recorded legacy a large portion of his work.

When war broke out, the Elgars were on holiday in Scotland. Among the places they visited was Iona, whose cathedral Alice found 'plain & distressingly *Protestant*'. Though the war curtailed musical activity, Elgar kept up his recording work. He managed a small amount of composition, too. While the public was rallying to 'Land of Hope and Glory', Elgar's personal thoughts were more subdued, as the elegiac *Sospiri* (for strings, harp, and organ), indicates. It was first performed at a promenade concert of patriotic music on 15 August 1914, but the 'sighs' of its Italian title reflect Elgar's mood. The composer was nothing if not a patriot (indeed, he wasted no time in joining the Special Constabulary when hostilities began), but he was upset by the xenophobia and unable to bear the brutality. He wrote to his friend Frank Schuster:

> Concerning the war I say nothing — the only thing that wrings my heart & soul is the thought of the horses — oh! my beloved animals — the men — and women can go to hell — but my horses; — I walk round & round this room cursing God for allowing dumb brutes to be tortured — let Him kill his human beings but — how CAN HE? Oh, my horses. (Moore 1984a: 670)

And Elgar, who had been understood and appreciated by the Germans long before his own countrymen, was distressed by the chauvinism and jingoism, particularly when his friends Sir Edgar and Lady Speyer (of German birth) were forced to leave the country. At one sparsely attended Elgar concert during the war, the absence of his supporters was explained in a nasty quip of Beecham's: 'They've all been interned'. Gestures from the German side distressed the Elgars too, especially Hans Richter's renunciation of his English honours. When the Three Choirs Festival was suspended until 1920, Lady Elgar blamed the 'Hun Kaiser'.

Significantly, his early 'war' works were written for the Belgians and the Polish. First came the recitation with music, *Carillon*, and this was followed between 1915 and 1917 by similar projects, *Une Voix dans le Désert* and *Le Drapeau Belge*. Most substantial was the 'symphonic prelude' *Polonia*, composed for a relief concert in aid of Ignace Paderewski's Polish Relief Fund.

Elgar sought escapism in writing music for *The Starlight Express*, a children's play by Algernon Blackwood which ran at the Kingsway Theatre early in 1916. The project fired Elgar's nostalgia for his youth, emotions only heightened by the war, and once again he went back to music of his childhood and *The Wand of Youth*. Public duties always loomed, though, and in March 1916 he completed *For the Fallen*, a Binyon setting for chorus and orchestra that was to become the final movement of a three-part elegy *The Spirit of England*, which he finished the following year. This is one of his finest scores of the period, and a work which the pacifist Britten admired particularly. Rather less significant, and more jingoistic, was his setting of Kipling poems, *The Fringes of the Fleet*, which was included as a part of a wartime variety bill at the London Coliseum during June 1917.

That year also saw Elgar compose his first (and only) ballet, *The Sanguine Fan*, which he conducted at the Chelsea Palace Theatre. But the war was taking its toll on Elgar's nerves and health, and the family decided to spend time out of London. A cottage called 'Brinkwells', near Fittleworth in West Sussex, was chosen, and the move proved to be a good one for the composer, bringing about an unprecedented late creative flowering. While recovering from a tonsil operation in early 1918, Elgar sketched the opening theme for what became the Cello Concerto. At the same time he began three pieces of chamber music, a genre with which he had struggled early in life. Now enjoying fame and a secure reputation, Elgar was at peace with himself, able to indulge his creative dreams. Within eighteen months he completed four of his most intimate, introspective works, all closely related in tonality and mood: the Violin Sonata and the String Quartet share the same key as the Cello Concerto, E minor, and the Piano Quintet is in A minor.

The first chamber work to be completed was the Violin Sonata, dedicated to a family friend Marie Joshua. The autumn and winter of 1918 were spent on the Quartet and Quintet; perhaps it is not too fanciful to suppose that the rural surroundings took Elgar back to his roots, since the Quintet uses a plainsong 'Salve regina' theme. All three works were premiered in the first half of 1919, and Elgar spent the summer completing the Cello Concerto. It was performed in October. Sadly, the premiere, like that of *Gerontius*, was a fiasco, largely the fault of Albert Coates, who conducted the rest of the programme. Coates's Russian musical sympathies meant that he devoted most of the rehearsal time to the other works in the programme, Borodin's Second Symphony and Scriabin's *Poem of Ecstasy*, at Elgar's expense. The public was already losing sympathy with Elgar's music, which they perceived to be out-of-date, and the concerto's reception was a bitter blow to the composer. In her diary, Lady Elgar labelled Coates 'a brutal, selfish, ill-mannered bounder'.

Alice herself was suffering ill-health. Within six months, on 7 April 1920, she died. Elgar noted in his diary for that day: 'My darling sinking. Father Valentine [from the Catholic Church in Hampstead] gave extreme unction. Sir Maurice [her doctor] called at 12.30. Sinking all day & died in my arms at 6.10 pm' (Moore 1984a: 752). In a quiet ceremony she was buried in the Catholic churchyard at Little Malvern. Philip Leicester recorded that 'E.E. seemed very grey, old, and grief-stricken. A big shock', and described the scene:

> All was quiet in the little church. The coffin lay solitary before the altar. The priest sat at the side. The score or so of mourners were still in their places. In the wee organ loft Will Reed and the three other members of the L.S.O. were playing the String Quartet. Very lovely and peaceful, the last tribute of the fiddlers. Then they buried her outside, close to the church.

At the beginning of May the composer wrote to his old friend Hubert Leicester:

> All thanks for your most kind letter & thank Agnes [Mrs Leicester] for hers also. I am still stunned & a weary broken man; but dear Carice is the greatest help & sees to everything. It was a great relief & happiness to be able to bury our dearest one in the sweet spot she chose herself. Would you very kindly convey one of the enclosed notices to the priest at Worcester, I do not think I know him, and ask that

it may be placed in the ususal way.

Elgar's will to compose diminished. Michael Kennedy has aptly described the years after 1920 as a period of 'creative sterility'. Elgar's marriage had brought his creative life into full focus, and he now missed Alice's assurance. He wrote to Ivor Atkins in 1922, referring to his works of the 1890s:

> It seems stange that the strong (it is *that*) characteristic stuff shd. have been conceived & written (by a poor wretch teaching all day) with a splitting headache after dinner & at odd, sustained moments... You, who like some of my work must thank *her* for all of it, not me. *I* should have destroyed it all & joined Job's wife in the congenial task of cursing God. (Moore 1984a: 209)

Not only had his wife's encouragement and practical help kept Elgar at his composition; her devotion had, in earlier years at least, kept Elgar to his faith. The personal catastrophe of war left him with a hopeless sense of despair and feelings of isolation, and Elgar lacked the spiritual inspiration to restore his optimism. His great friend W.H. Reed wrote of the composer's outlook in 1925:

> He never talked about his religion; but he was obviously more sceptical generally as a widower than he had been during Lady Elgar's lifetime... (Reed 1936: 74-75)

Arnold Bax was more emphatic and claimed that Elgar 'became cranky and embittered' (Bax: 32). According to George Bernard Shaw, Elgar evaded the subject of religion with a deliberate reticence and was 'a nineteeth-century unbeliever, though he wouldn't have admitted it and wouldn't have liked to be told so' (Pearson: 392).

Perhaps Newman was most perceptive when he wrote in the *Sunday Times* years later:

> His Catholicism seemed to me to be in large part the product of the impact on him from boyhood onwards of all the magnificent art that Christian emotion had called into being throughout so many centuries. And so, when put to a sharply realistic test his religion, I think, was apt to give him scant support. (*Sunday Times* 6/6/55)

What remained of Elgar's Catholicism was sentimental associations, as this touching letter written on 15 December 1924 to Hubert Leicester's wife, Agnes, indicates:

> I must send you one line to thank you for all the trouble you took over the disposal of dear Alice's poor old pianoforte. As I said this morning, it is best that it should go to Dot [Elgar's sister] — the Rev. Mother General(!) — for her school & so it will end its feeble days, as my dearest wd. have wished, in a Catholic instituition.

Elgar's spiritual crisis was compounded by the national upheaval of the war. The lives of a whole generation had been disrupted by the huge destruction, but Elgar was also, as the country became increasingly industrialized, witnessing the erosion of the visionary England he held dear.

For Elgar it was to be a time of wandering. He had never felt at home in Severn House, Hampstead, and his finances forced him to give it up in 1921. Leaving the house meant much clearing out, and many manuscripts — in all likelihood, early church music among them — were destroyed. Carice noted 'Father went though all his sketches, M.S.S. etc sad work. Destroyed much & got all in order' (Anderson: 149). Old angers resurfaced when his economic situation was brought home to him by Alice's aunts, who, in a fit of class snobbery, had ensured that none of the Roberts inheritance should go to descendents of Elgar. He wrote to Schuster:

> I am plunged in the midst of ancient hate & prejudice — poor dear A's settlements & her *awful aunts* who wd. allow nothing to descend to any offspring of *mine* — I had forgotten all the petty bitterness but I feel just now rather evil that... my Carice should be penalised by a wretched lot of old incompetents simply because I was — well — I.

After Carice married Samuel Blake on 16 January 1922 at St James, Spanish Place, Elgar spent an increasing amount of time in his clubs, conveniently located near the small flat he had taken in St James's Place. He composed nothing, but music was not completely ignored — he continued conducting and recording. When he could no longer keep away from manuscript paper, he turned to arranging. He provided a sumptuous, exuberant orchestration of Bach's Fantasia and Fugue in C Minor *BWV* 537 (an organ work he had played in his St George's days), and a year later treated a Handel overture in the same way for the Worcester Three Choirs Festival. About the Handel (from the second Chandos Anthem), Elgar wrote to John West of Novello in July 1923: 'I have known the overture from the two old stave organ accompaniment since I was a little boy and always wanted it to be heard in a large form — the weighty structure is (to me) so grand — epic' (Moore 1987: 828). Anthems received orchestrated accompaniments too: Parry's *Jerusalem* (1922), Battishill's *O Lord, look down from heaven* (1923) and S.S. Wesley's *Let us lift up our hearts* (1923).

Elgar returned to composition proper for the first time in three years with incidental music to Laurence Binyon's *Arthur*, first performed at the Old Vic on 23 March 1923. That spring he was at last able to move back to Worcestershire. He took Napleton Grange at Kempsey, on the River Severn just south of Worcester. But he remained restless, and in November he was off again, on a voyage up the Amazon. He sailed in the 'Hildebrand' from Liverpool via Madiera to South America, and a thousand miles up the Amazon to Manoas. Little is known of his impressions, though he was full of admiration for the way in which a Brazilian town of reasonable size could boast a handsome opera house. That in Manoas, built by rubber barons only a few years before, was especially impressive.

Back home in 1924, he was appointed to succeed Sir Walter Parratt as Master of the King's Musick, and it fell to him to provide an *Empire March* and *The Pageant of Empire* for the British Empire Exhibition at Wembley Stadium. Elgar did not enjoy the experience. Beneath the public façade, he was overwhelmed by the etiquette and vulgarity of the occasion, as he wrote to Alice Stuart-Wortley: '17,000 men, hammering, loud speakers, amplifiers — four aeroplanes circling over etc. etc. — all mechanical & horrible — no soul & no romance & no imagination' (Moore 1984a: 769). His composition of these two works did not signal a return of his full creative powers. From 1925 until 1929 only a few pieces appeared, two part-songs, two carols (see below), incidental music for *Beau Brummel*, a Civic Fanfare for the opening of the Hereford Three Choirs Festival in 1927, and another arrangement (Purcell's anthem *Jehova*, *quam multi sunt*).

During the 1926 Worcester Festival extracts from Wagner's *Parsifal* were included in the programme, much to the chagrin of a member of the cathedral clergy, Canon Lacey. His attack in the *Worcester Daily Times* on the planned performance drew a swift response from Elgar on 17 March : 'As to the "delirium of sensual love and that craving for the refreshing ministrations of the white-robed angels", has Canon Lacey forgotten John Donne who, after experiencing the same travail, ended his life in the same Church of England of which Canon Lacey is such a distinguished, if a somewhat disingenuous, ornament'.

Elgar was reaching seventy, and apart from his conducting and (extensive) recording commitments, what mattered most to him was the countryside. While he socialised frequently in London, he was most content with gatherings of friends at the Three Choirs Festival each year. It is interesting that very few of the composer's co-religionists were among his intimate circle. Indeed, one feature of Christianity which contributed most to Elgar's distress was the prominent sectarianism of his day, and his concern at such divisions is shown in the letter of congratulation he wrote on 22 February 1927 to the Archbishop of Canterbury, Randall Davidson, on the occasion of his twenty-five years as Primate:

> Bred in another form of religious observance I stand aside, unbiased, from the trivialities with which controversies are mostly informed; whatever differences exist there remains the clear, wide and refreshing Christianity, desired by all men but obscured by the little darkness of their own imperfect vision. To the better understanding of such broad Christian feeling I am thankful to have been permitted, in a small way it is true, to exercise my art; in this spirit and in a spirit of humble fellowship I offer this tribute of deep respect — to an ideal great churchman, a staunch friend and an embodiment of all that is good & true in Christianity past mere forms & observances. (Young 1955: 230)

Only towards the end of his life did two small church works appear. Characterized by a new simplicity, they may have been part of a conscious effort to rekindle the past and his early days at St George's Catholic Church. The first was a carol set to verses by

Ben Jonson, *I sing the birth was born tonight* (Appendix One: 3.6). (He turned to Jonson again four years later, for an operatic subject.)

Elgar was evidently anticipating Christmas when he wrote the carol at Tiddington House, near Stratford-upon-Avon, shortly after the Gloucester Festival of 1928. Elgar sent his setting to the publishers on the day of completion (30 October) and they offered him fifteen guineas for the copyright. He replied on 1 November:

> I am obliged to you for the letter as to the B. Jonson Carol. I accept your offer. I took the words from *Gifford's* edn which is authentic & I do not think has been superseded by any modern edition, but the spelling is modernised: if you prefer the original — which might *look* well — I can easily get the first version[.] But you are the best judges of the *utility* of quaint spelling[.] (Moore 1987: 858)

The modernised spelling was preferred by the publishers.

The first performance was given by the Royal Choral Society in the Royal Albert Hall on 10 December 1928, under the direction of Malcolm Sargent. Before long it was performed for a second time, by Ivor Atkins at Evensong in Worcester Cathedral on 26 December 1928.

I sing the birth is modal and largely constructed of single lines; Elgar directs in the score that 'These passages should be sung in a very free manner, without any rigid adherence to *tempo*'. In its austere modality and free treatment it resembles settings in a similar style by Holst and Vaughan Williams. Perhaps it was the aging Elgar's attempt to come to terms with the new asceticism of the younger generation of composers or a passing flirtation with the current folk-song revival, but it is more likely to have been suggested by the modality of plainsong — a way of calling up his Catholic origins. Its economy and simplicity are of a kind hardly encountered in Elgar's earlier output, but point to the new directions revealed in the Soliliquy for Oboe (1930) and the sketches for the Third Symphony. Except for two verses sung by the whole choir, this carol is shaped in long unaccompanied solo lines, interspersed with modal 'Alleluias'.

Elgar produced his last 'church' work, *Good Morrow* (Appendix One: 3.7), in response to a request from Sir Walford Davies, the organist of St George's Chapel, Windsor Castle. (Walford Davies, a Shrewsbury man of Welsh extraction, was one of the few composers with whom Elgar had a close friendship; it dated from at least the turn of the century.) The intention was for a piece to celebrate the King's recovery, in autumn 1929, from his first serious illness. Plans had been made for Elgar to provide a piece for *The King's Book*, a commemorative publication with contributions from distinguished figures. Nothing came of this collaboration and eventually Elgar celebrated the monarch's recovery in his own way, subtitling his work 'A simple Carol for His Majesty's happy recovery'.

Walford Davies's request, dated 6 June 1919, was for 'such a work that we could sing to the King and record for public consumption' ('Young 1956: 300). It was not until some months later that Elgar submitted to him the text he had chosen. He enclosed Gascoigne's 'You that have spent the silent night' for Walford Davies's approval in a letter dated 31 October 1929 written at Stratford-upon-Avon:

> I enclose some words by old Gascoigne. let [sic] me know if they will do: the 'affair' is quite a simple tune &, I need not say, not worthy of your occasion but it might be appropriate in a mild sense. I propose to put a sub-title 'A simple carol for H.M.'s recovery' — but Carol has perhaps a narrow meaning: send me the words back & I am quite prepared for you, dear friend, to say it will not do. Just a simple tune that's all[.] (Young 1956: 300-301)

Before long, on 6 November, Elgar offered the work to Novello:

> I have a *Partsong Carol* sort of thing
>
> > 'A simple Carol for His Majesty's happy recovery'
>
> & it has struck me that you might care to issue it in the Decr. *Musical Times*. Sir Walford Davies will perform it for the first time on *Decr 9th*. at the St. G's Choir Concert in *Windsor* which I conduct & which will be broadcast. (Moore 1987: 865)

On 8 November the publishers offered the composer a fee of ten guineas and a royalty of fifteen per cent, which he accepted. On the same day he reported developments to Walford Davies:

> Novello has sent the M.S. of the little affair & will have copies ready for you very shortly: let me know how many you will require. I wish you cd. record it! & possibly 'Ave Verum' on the reverse. And Novello's wish to put something like —
>
> 'First performed by the St. George's Choir, Windsor, at their Annual Concert 9th Dec 1929'??
>
> Will you like an angel let me have the correct wording for this? Can't I get you name into it?
>
> I shd. love to do so (Young 1956: 301)

As it happened, *Good Morrow* was not recorded, though the performance which Elgar conducted at Windsor on 9 December was broadcast. Two days later Elgar sent copies of the carol to Sir Frederick Ponsonby, Keeper of the Privy Purse, who acknowledged them:

> The King desires me to thank you for the copies of the Carol which you have been good enough to write on His Majesty's recovery. The King is taking these copies down to Sandringham and intends to ask the choir to sing your carol. (De-la-Noy: 204)

Elgar adapted an early hymn tune of his for use in *Good Morrow*. The hymn 'Praise ye the Lord: on ev'ry height' was originally set in C major when Elgar wrote it in 1878 (see pp.35-36), but here it is re-arranged in B-flat. The source upon which Elgar drew is revealed in letters to Hubert Leicester, who had retained many of the manuscripts dating from Elgar's days at St George's. Elgar's letter is dated 29 July 1929, not long after Walford Davies' request:

> Do you think you cd. find a copy of the old *'Hymns for the Year'*? I want to see the words of 'Praise['] — (something about praise anyway) as I wish to make use of the tune I wrote. (BL Add MS 60357: f. 205)

Leicester obliged him and Elgar returned the music on 6 August:

> Thank you for sending the old Hymn which I return with this: the tune I think may be used for festive occasions but of that we shall decide later. (BL Add MS 60357: f. 207)

EDWARD ELGAR: SACRED MUSIC

In its original key of C major, the tune went too high for comfortable singing; the transposition down made it a little more manageable. Naturally, Elgar made some other refinements. Harmonically, verse one remains closest to the original. Each of the five verses is slightly different in texture: in verse three, for example, the 'little birds' are represented by the sopranos and altos (divided) only and through quaver movement, and the 'rainbow bending in the sky' of verse five is depicted in the three upper parts only.

Elgar's setting was of verses by the Tudor poet George Gascoigne. Although many of the younger generation of English composers were turning to such sources, Elgar was not normally inclined to set texts of this period. The words are naive, but Elgar captures their simple spirituality effectively, in a setting that again reflects his nostalgia during these years. The early hymn tune would have called up his Worcestershire childhood and his beginings at St George's.

Elgar's insecurity had been increased by moves from Napleton Grange to a house on the outskirts of Worcester, from there to Stratford-upon-Avon, and finally, in 1929, to Marl Bank in Worcester, where he remained for the rest of his life. For the Three Choirs Festival at Worcester that year, Ivor Atkins tried to persuade Elgar to produce a new work. The composer came up with the idea of choral settings of two Shelley poems, 'Adonais' and 'The daemon of the world', but the Cathedral's Dean rejected them as 'frankly pagan' — hardly surprising, considering the anti-clerical references in 'The daemon'. 'Adonais' does seem to have summed up Elgar's position then:

> The breath whose might I have invoked in song
> Descends on me; my spirit's bark is driven,
> Far from the shore, far from the trembling throng
> Whose sails were never to the tempest given;
> The massy earth and spherèd skies are riven!
> I am borne darkly, fearfully, afar...

Elgar's Christmas card that year took a quotation from Walt Whitman:

> I think I could turn and live with animals, they are so
>   placid and self-contain'd;

They do not sweat and whine about their condition;
They do not lie awake in the dark and weep for their sins;
They do not make me sick discussing their duty to God;
Not one is dissatisfied — not one demented with the mania
  of owning things;
Not one kneels to another, nor to his kind that lived
  thousands of years ago;
Not one is respectable or industrious over the whole earth.

At Marl Bank, as the new decade dawned, Elgar became more deeply engrossed in his composition, though more often that not old sketchbooks were raided for inspiration. In 1930, apart from a fifth (and final) *Pomp and Circumstance* March which Elgar added to the set, the major work was the *Severn Suite*, dedicated to George Bernard Shaw. It was written for brass band, and later orchestrated by Elgar and arranged as the Organ Sonata No. 2 by Ivor Atkins. Each of the four movements depicts a Worcester riverside scene. When Elgar was less than ten years old he had been found on the banks of the Severn with pencil and manuscript paper, 'trying to write down what the reeds were saying'. He remained throughout his life, as he put it to his friend Sidney Colvin, 'at heart the dreamy child who used to be found in the reeds by Severn side...'.

Themes from early sketches of the 1870s and 1880s found their way into the *Nursery Suite* of 1931. The most direct quotaton comes in the first movement, 'Aubade', which takes the hymn tune from 1878, later set to 'Hear Thy children, gentle Jesus' (see p. 36). The work, in much the same vein as the *Wand of Youth* suites and *The Starlight Express*, was the last composition of any size he completed. It was recorded in the middle of the year, within a few weeks of Elgar's being made a Baronet. 1932 and 1933 saw a few piano pieces and some choral songs, but there were three big projects on his mind: a piano concerto, a third symphony and an opera.

Not for the first time, Elgar was toying with the idea of a piano concerto. He had been sketching such a work on and off since 1909, but in the end it came to nothing. The Third Symphony progressed much further: under pressure from George Bernard Shaw, Elgar persuaded the BBC to commission the piece, and he began it full of enthusiasm, but it remained incomplete at the time of his death.

Indeed, the extent of the work he left aroused some controversy at the time. In all probability Elgar lacked the will to carry it through, and in any case before long illness was to impede work.

There was one other distraction, his projected opera *The Spanish Lady*. Elgar had entertained a life-long enthusiasm for opera, but the genre was one towards which the English musical establishment was hostile. Both Strauss and Richter had encouraged Elgar to compose one, he had discussed the possibility of collaboration with Shalyapin (a *King Lear*), and corresponded with Thomas Hardy about a suitable subject (*The Tempest*, *The Return of the Native*, or a section of *The Dynasts*). In 1932, however, he set his mind on Ben Jonson's *The Devil is an Ass*, and began working with his librettist, Sir Barry Jackson, in earnest. Some sections progressed well, were copied over and over again, played to his friends; unusually, the composer even sketched a stage design. Elgar's plans were ambitious, but it is doubtful if they could ever have been fulfilled. The surviving music has charm but little sense of drama; indeed, earlier oratorios and canatas suggest that Elgar was happier reporting drama than portraying it. In May 1933 Elgar went to France (flying by aeroplane for the first time, a sensation that thrilled him), where he met Delius, a happy occasion at which champagne and mutual admiration flowed. Events elsewhere in Europe distressed him, as he wrote to Adela Schuster: 'I am in a maze regarding events in Germany — what are they doing? In this morning's paper it is said that the greatest conductor Bruno Walter &, stranger still, Einstein, are ostracised: are we all mad? The Jews have always been my best & kindest friends — the pain of these news is unbearable & I do not know what it really means' (Moore 1984a: 809).

For Elgar, too, there was bad news. Shortly after the Hereford Three Choirs Festival in autumn 1933, he was diagnosed as suffering from cancer. Dr Arthur Thompson, the consultant in whom Elgar confided during his illness, told Jerrold Northrop Moore in 1976 that the composer had no faith whatsoever in an afterlife: 'I believe there is nothing but complete oblivion,' Elgar is reported to have said (Moore 1984a: 818). Towards the end of his life Elgar was reluctant to see a priest, saying that he objected to the church's 'mumbo-jumbo' (Kennedy: 328). Philip Leicester, another visitor, and a devout Catholic, was shocked to hear Elgar's request to be cremated. Eventually, though, Carice persuaded him otherwise. Shortly before his death, Elgar was visited by Fr Reginald Gibb from St George's Catholic Church, and the last rites were administered. According to Fr Gibb, he obtained a confession of faith from the frail Elgar. (A letter [dated 18 November 1968, now at the Jesuit Archives, Farm Street, London] from Carice Elgar Blake to Fr Kelly, then Parish Priest at St George's Catholic Church, Worcester, confirms that Fr Gibb saw the dying Elgar, who did reaffirm his faith in the Roman Catholic Church.) We cannot be certain what Elgar believed. Since music, even that in *The Dream of Gerontius*, can never be theologically explicit, the mystery of his religious convictions will remain another unsolved enigma.

* * * *

Elgar died early in the morning of 23 February 1934. He was buried three days later in the churchyard at St Wulstan's, Little Malvern, in a simple ceremony without music. George Bernard Shaw wrote that 'of all composers Elgar is alone for Westminster Abbey', but Elgar's remains were laid to rest at home in Worcestershire, next to his wife's: the 'outsider' had returned home.

Simultaneously, a Low Requiem Mass was said at St George's Catholic Church, Worcester, where his *Pie Jesu* of 1887 was sung. On 2 March a memorial service was held in a packed Worcester Cathedral, where a choir and the London Symphony Orchestra paid tribute to him with music which included excerpts from *The Dream of Gerontius*. Ironically, this recognition came in the same Anglican Cathedral where, in 1902, objections had been raised to a performance of a work so full of Roman Catholic theology.

Appendix One

1.1 Kyrie Eleison (p. 18)

Date of composition:	Undated [c. 1868-1869]
Setting:	SATB
Manuscript source:	In private possession
Key:	A major
Number of bars:	20

1.2 Gloria (p. 19)

Date of composition: Undated [c. 1872-1873]
Setting: SATB, soloists, organ.
Manuscript sources:
A) Score: BL Add MS 49973A: ff. 97-127
B) Vocal score: BL Add MS 49973A: ff. 128-130v
C) Individual vocal parts:
   Soprano solo & tutti: BL Add MS 49973A: ff.131-132v
   Alto: BL Add MS 49973A: ff.133-134
   Tenor: BL Add MS 49973A: ff.135-136
   Bass: BL Add MS 49973A: ff.137-138
   Bass solo: BL Add MS 49973A: ff.139-140v

Key: F major
Tempo: Allegro
Number of bars: 185

APPENDIX ONE

1.3 Credo (p. 20)

Date of composition:	July 1873
Setting:	SATB, soloists, organ
Manuscript sources:	A) BL Add MS 63163
	B) Jesuit Archives MS 52/2/2/2
Key:	Various; opens in A minor and ends in A major
Tempi:	Various
Number of bars:	306

1.4 Introduction to an unidentified anthem (p. 23)

Date of composition:	1874
Setting:	Strings
Manuscript source:	BL Add MS 49973A: f. 88v.
Key:	B flat major
Number of bars:	17

1.5 Salve Regina (p. 24)

Date of composition:	1876
Setting:	SATB, soloists, organ
Opus number:	none (but originally termed Op. 1)
Manuscript sources:	A) BL Add MS 49973A ff. 22-27
	B) Jesuit Archives MS 52/2/2/1
	C) Birthplace Museum: MS 93
Key:	D major
Tempi:	Allegro moderato; Moderato; Adagio
Number of bars:	141

EDWARD ELGAR: SACRED MUSIC

1.6 Tantum ergo (p. 25)

Date of composition:	1876
Setting:	SATB, soloists, organ
Opus number:	None (but originally termed Op. 2)
Manuscript sources:	A) BL Add MS 49973A: ff. 15-18v
	B) Jesuit Archives MS 52/2/2/1
	C) Birthplace MS 93
First performance:	21 June 1879, St George's Catholic Church, Worcester
Key:	D major
Tempi:	Andante; Adagio; Allegro maestoso
Number of bars:	Source A: 77 bars (Four extra bars indicated at the end of Source B)

1.7 Regina Coeli (p.26)

Date of composition:	Undated [c.1876]
Setting:	SATB, soprano solo, organ
Manuscript source:	Jesuit Archives MS 52/2/1, MS 52/2/2/1
Key:	F major
Tempi:	Moderato, Allegro, Andante, Allegro, [Andante]
Number of bars:	46 (incomplete — last section not in manuscript)

1.8 Psalm 84 (p. 26)

Date of composition:	c.1876
Setting:	Soprano solo and organ
Manuscript source:	BL Add MS 64061 B: f. 31
Key:	A major
Tempo :	All[egr]o Vivace
Number of bars:	Incomplete manuscript

APPENDIX ONE

1.9 Gloria (p. 28)

Date of composition:	1877
Setting:	S[A?]TB, organ
Manuscript source:	Jesuit Archive 52/2/2/1 (soprano and tenor parts only)
Key:	C major
Tempo:	All[egr]o Spiritoso
Number of bars:	172

1.10 Kyrie Eleison (p. 28)

Date of composition:	Undated [c. 1877]
Setting:	STB, organ
Manuscript sources:	A) Jesuit Archive 52/2/2/1
	B) Birthplace Museum MS 94
Key:	D minor
Tempo:	Adagio
Number of bars:	123

1.11 Credo (p. 28)

Date of composition:	1877, perhaps earlier
Setting:	SATB, organ
Opus number:	None (but originally termed Op. 3)
Manuscript source:	BL Add MS 49973A: ff. 29-35
Key:	E minor
Tempi:	[no indication at beginning], Andante, Allegro molto, A tempo
Number of bars:	190

1.12 O Salutaris Hostia (p. 31)

Date of composition:	Undated [c. 1877]
Setting:	Contralto solo, organ
Manuscript sources:	A) Birthplace Museum: MS 75
	B) BL Add MS 63146
Key:	G major
Tempo:	[Andantino]
Number of bars:	53

1.13 O Salutaris Hostia (p. 32)

Date of composition:	Undated [c. 1877-1878]
Setting:	either a) SATB and organ or b) soprano and organ
Manuscript source:	Jesuit Archives MS 52/2/2/1
Key:	E minor
Tempo:	Adagio
Number of bars:	16, but incomplete

1.14 Credo (p. 33)

Date of composition:	Undated [c.1878]
Setting:	S[ATB, organ]
Manuscript source:	BL Add MS 63146: f. 15
Key:	G major
Number of bars:	21; incomplete sketch

1.15 Kyrie Eleison (p. 33)

Date of composition:	Undated [c. 1878]
Setting:	SATB, organ
Manuscript source:	BL Add MS 63147: f. 7

APPENDIX ONE

Key: C minor
Number of bars: Incomplete sketch

1.16 Sanctus (p. 33)

Date of composition: Undated [c. 1878]
Setting: [SATB]
Manuscript source: BL Add MS 63147: f. 11
Key: [C major]
Number of bars: Incomplete fragment

1.17 Magnificat (p. 34)

Date of composition: Undated [c.1878]
Setting: SATB, organ
Manuscript source: BL Add MS 63147: f. 15v.
Key: G major
Tempo: Mod[era]to
Number of bars: Incomplete sketch

1.18 Hymn tune (p. 37)

First line (text); Now with the fast departing light
Date of composition: 16 June 1878
Manuscript source: BL Add MS 63146: ff. 19v., 20
Key: G major
Number of bars: 16
Metre: 8.8.8.8.

1.19 Hymn tune (p. 37)

First line (text):	Hear Thy children gentle Jesus
Date of composition:	21 July 1878
Manuscript sources:	A) BL Add MS 63146: f. 19
	B) Birthplace Museum MS 58
	C) Jesuit Archives MSS 52/2/2/8, 52/2/2/9, 52/2/2/10 (part-books)
First published:	*The Catholic Hymnal* (1896)
Key:	F major
Number of bars:	8
Metre:	8.7.8.7.

1.20 Hymn tune (p. 37)

First line (text):	Praise ye the Lord: on ev'ry height
Date of composition:	Undated [c.1878]
Manuscript sources:	A) BL Add MS 63146: f. 17v.
	B) BL Add MS 63147: f. 1
	C) Birthplace Museum MS 49
	D) Jesuit Archives MS 52/2/2/10, MS 52/2/2/8
	E) BL Add MS 63149: f. 20v.
Key:	C major
Number of bars:	30
Metre:	8.6.14.14.13.

1.21 Hymn tune (p. 37)

First line (text):	Unknown
Date of composition:	Undated [c. 1878]
Manuscript source:	BL Add MS 49973A: f. 20
Key:	G major
Number of bars:	12
Metre:	10.10.12.8.4.

APPENDIX ONE

1.22 Hymn tune (p. 37)

First line (text):	By the blood that flowed from Thee
Date of composition:	Undated [c.1878]
Manuscript source:	BL Add MS 49973A: ff. 11, 12
Key:	E flat major
Number of bars:	32
Metre:	7.7.7.7.7.7.7.7.

1.23 Magnificat (p. 34)

Date of composition:	Undated [c. 1878-1879]
Setting:	SATB, organ
Manuscript sources:	A) BL Add MS 63147: f. 21
	B) BL Add MS 63148: ff. 19v., 20
Key:	F major
Number of bars:	Incomplete manuscript

1.24 Domine Salvum Fac (p. 34)

Date of composition:	1879
Manuscript source:	BL Add MS 63149 ff. 18-20
First performance:	21 June 1879, St George's Catholic Church, Worcester
Key:	D major
Tempo:	Allegro
Number of bars:	Incomplete
Setting:	SATB, strings and winds

1.25 Gloria (p. 33)

Date of composition:	Undated [c.1879]
Setting:	SATB, organ

EDWARD ELGAR: SACRED MUSIC

Manuscript source: BL Add MS 63149: ff. 11v., 12
Key: G major
Number of bars: Incomplete sketch

1.26 Brother, for thee He died (p. 35)

Date of composition: 1879
Setting: Bass solo, organ
Manuscript source: BL Add MS 63149: f. 28v.
Key: D minor
Tempo: Beginning unmarked, Allegretto section appears later
Number of bars: Incomplete manuscript

1.27 Chant

Date of composition: Undated [c.1879]
Manuscript source: BL Add MS 63149: f. 20v.
Key: G minor
Number of bars: 5

1.28 Hymn tune (p. 38)

First line (text):   Unknown
Date of composition: Undated [c.1879]
Manuscript source: BL Add MS 63149 f. 28
Key: A flat major
Number of bars: 12
Metre: 7.7.7.7.7.7.7.

APPENDIX ONE

1.29 Hymn tune (p. 42)

First line (text):	O Salutaris Hostia
Date of composition:	Undated [c.1880 or earlier]
Manuscript source:	BL Add MS 49973A: f. 94
Key:	E flat major
Number of bars:	24 (20 + 4 for 'Amen')
Metre:	8.8.8.8.

1.30 O Salutaris Hostia (p. 39)

Date of composition:	c.1880
Setting:	SATB, organ
First published:	Alphonse Cary, 1889
Manuscript source:	BL Add MS 49973 A ff. 87, 87v., 88
Key:	E flat major
Tempo:	Andante
Number of bars:	35 (MS = 41 bars)

1.31 Gloria (p. 42)

Date of composition:	Undated [c.1881]
Setting:	SATB, organ
Manuscript source:	BL Add MS 63150: f. 3v.
Key:	D major
Number of bars:	Incomplete manuscript

1.32 O Salutaris Hostia (p. 41)

Date of composition:	17 April 1882
Setting:	Bass solo, chorus ad lib., organ
Manuscript sources:	A) Score: BL Add MS 63164
	B) Chorus part: BL Add MS 49973A: f. 86

Key: E flat major
Tempo: Andantino
Number of bars: 77

1.33 Kyrie Eleison (p. 42)

Date of composition: Undated [c.1882]
Manuscript source: BL Add MS 63164: f. 2v.
Key: C major
Number of bars: Incomplete sketch

1.34 Benedictus (p.43)

Date of composition: 7 May 1882
Setting: SATB, strings and organ
Manuscript source: BL Add MS 63150: ff. 17v.-18v.
Key: G major
Number of bars: 58

1.35 O Salutaris Hostia (p. 40)

Date of composition: c.1880-1888
Setting: SATB, organ
Manuscript source: Unknown
First published: Cary, 1898
Key: F major
Tempo: Poco Adagio
Number of bars: 19 (with repeats 34)

APPENDIX ONE

1.36 Hymn tune (p. 46)

First line (text):	Stabat Mater dolorosa
Date of composition:	March 1886
Manuscript sources:	A) BL Add MS 49973A: ff. 9, 10
	B) Birthplace Museum MS 58
Key:	F major
Number of bars:	8 (6 + 2 for 'Amen')
Metre:	8.8.8.

1.37 Litany Chants (p. 46)

Date of composition:	Mostly c.1876-1886
Manuscript sources:	A) In private possession
	B) In private possession
	C) Birthplace Museum MS 96
	D) Birthplace Museum MS 95
First published:	Cary: 'Four Litanies of the Blessed Virgin Mary', 1888
Keys:	Various

1.38 Ave Verum (p. 48)
(originally Pie Jesu)

Date of composition:	Pie Jesu: 28 January 1887, revised as Ave Verum 1902
Setting:	SATB, organ
Opus number:	Op. 2 No. 1
Manuscript sources:	*Pie Jesu:*
	A) BL Add MS 49973A: f. 84
	B) BL Add MS 49973A: f. 90
	C) BL Add MS 49973A: f. 93
First published:	Novello, 1902
Current edition:	Novello
Key:	G major

Tempo: Largo
Number of bars: 39

1.39 Ave Maria (p.49)

Date of composition: [c.1887] revised 1907
Setting: SATB, organ
Opus number: Op. 2 No. 2
First published: Novello, 1907
Current edition: Novello
Manuscript source: Unknown
Key: B flat major
Tempo: Andantino
Number of bars: 31

1.40 Ave Maris Stella (p. 49)

Date of composition: [c.1887] revised 1907
Setting: SATB, organ
Opus number: Op. 2 No. 3
First published: Novello, 1907
Current edition: Novello
Manuscript source: Unknown
Key: G major
Tempo: Lento
Number of bars: 69

1.41 Ecce Sacerdos Magnus (p. 52)

Date of composition: 1888
Setting: SATB, organ
Manuscript sources: (A) Jesuit Archives MS 52/2/1
(B) BL Add MS 58054: ff. 1-30v.

APPENDIX ONE

First published: Cary, 1888
First performance: 9 October 1888, St George's Catholic Church, Worcester
Key: G major
Tempo: Andante Maestoso
Number of bars: 53

2.1 Te Deum and Benedictus in F (p. 62)

Date of composition: 1897
Setting: Chorus (SATB) and orchestra or organ
Opus number: 34
Manuscript sources: A) Sketches: BL Add MS 58048: ff. 1-30
B) Orchestral score: BL Add MS 57999
First published: Novello 1897
Current edition: Novello
First performance: 12 September 1897, Hereford Festival
Key: F major
Tempi: Various
Number of bars: Te Deum = 228; Benedictus = 118

2.2 Carol for Christmastide (p. 66)
(originally Grete Malverne on a rocke)

First line (text): Lo! Christ the Lord is born
Date of composition: 1897
Manuscript source: Unknown
First published: Novello, 1909
Key: F major
Number of bars: 16
Tempo: Allegretto

2.3 Hymn tune (p. 72)

First line (text):	O Mightiest of the mighty
Date of composition:	January 1902
Manuscript source:	BL Add MS 63153: f. 15
First published:	Novello, 1902
Key:	C major
Number of bars:	21 (including 'Alleluia' and 'Amen')
Tempo:	Allegro

2.4 Anthem (p. 73)

Date of composition:	Undated [1903-1910?]
Manuscript source:	BL Add MS 63159: ff. 25v., 26
Key:	E flat major / C minor
Number of bars:	Incomplete sketch

2.5 Two Single Chants for Venite (p. 82)

Date of composition:	1907
Manuscript source:	A) BL Add MS 63157: f. 1v.
	B) BL Add MS 69827: f. 36
First published:	Novello: 'The New Cathedral Psalter' (Nos. 155 and 167), 1909
Key:	1) G major (No. 167), 2) D major (No. 155)
Number of bars:	7 bars each

2.6 Two Double Chants: 1)Psalm 68 2)Psalm 75 (p. 82)

Date of composition:	1907
Manuscript source:	A) BL Add MS 63157: f. 2
	B) BL Add MS 69827: f. 36
First published:	Novello: 'The New Cathedral Psalter' (nos. 156 and 168), 1909

APPENDIX ONE

Key: Both in D major
Number of bars: Both 14 bars long

2.7 Psalm Chants (p. 83)

Date of composition: 1907
Manuscript source: BL Add MS 63157: f. 3
Key: 1) A minor 2) C minor
Number of bars: 1) 7 bars 2) 14 bars

2.8 Angelus (p. 85)

Date of composition: 1909
Setting: SATB unaccompanied
Opus number: Op. 56 No. 1
Manuscript source: Sketches: BL Add MS 63161; BL Add MS 63159, f. 19; BL Add MS 63157, f. 19
First performance: 8 December 1910, Royal Albert Hall, London.
Key: E flat major
Tempo: Allegretto
Number of bars: 84

2.9 They are at Rest (p. 87)

Date of composition: 1909
Setting: SATB unaccompanied
Manuscript source: Unknown
First published: Novello, 1910
Current edition: Novello
First performance: 22 January 1910, Royal Mausoleum, Frogmore
Key: D major

EDWARD ELGAR: SACRED MUSIC

Tempo: Lento e sostenuto
Number of bars: 26
Text author: Cardinal Newman

3.1 O Hearken Thou (p. 90)

Date of composition:	1911
Setting:	SATB, orchestra; accompaniment arranged for organ by Elgar
Opus number:	Op.64
Manuscript sources:	A) Sketches: BL Add MS 47907A: ff.138-141
	B) Vocal score: BL Add MS 58049: ff. 5-7
First published:	Novello, 1911
Current edition:	Novello
First performance:	22 June 1911, Coronation of King George V, Westminster Abbey
Key:	A flat major
Tempo:	Molto Lento ed expressivo
Number of bars:	28 (version with two verses = 50 bars)

3.2 Great is the Lord (p. 92)

Date of composition:	24 August 1910 - March 1912
Setting:	SATB with divisions, bass solo; organ (orchestrated 1913)
Opus number:	Op. 67
Manuscript sources:	A) Sketches: BL Add MS 47907A: ff. 159-168
	B) Vocal score: BL Add MS 58034: ff. 2-40
	C) Orchestration: BL Add MS 58035: ff. 1-19
First published:	Novello, 1912
Current edition:	Novello
First performance:	16 July 1912, Westminster Abbey

APPENDIX ONE

Key: D major
Tempi: Moderato; Allegro moderato; Maestoso;
                           Andante; Andantino; Moderato pui maestoso
Number of bars: 209

3.3 Give unto the Lord (p. 97)

Date of composition: January - March 1914
Setting: SATB (with divisions) and organ, orchestrated April 1914
Opus number: Op. 74
Manuscript sources: A) Sketches: BL Add MS 47908: ff. 106-130
                           B) Fragment: BL Add MS 63154: f. 67v.
                           C) Vocal score: BL Add MS 58034: ff. 41-72
                           D) Revised proofs: Birthplace PR 49
First published: Novello, 1914
Current edition: Novello
First performance: 30 April 1914, St Paul's Cathedral, London
Key: E♭ major
Tempi: Maestoso; Allegro moderato; Pui tranquillo; Molto maestoso
Number of bars: 142

3.4 Fear Not, O land (p. 100)

Date of composition: 1914
Setting: SATB, organ
Manuscript sources: A) Sketches: BL Add MS 47908: ff. 76-179
                           B) Vocal score: BL Add MS 69827: ff. 38-45 (unbound: provisional numbering in

	1993)
First published:	Novello, 1914
Current edition:	Novello
Key:	F major
Tempo:	Allegretto moderato
Number of bars:	101

3.5 Hymn tune (p. 101)

First line (text):	O Perfect Love
Date of composition:	22 June 1914
Manuscript source:	Birthplace Museum MS 85
Key:	F major
Number of bars:	16
Metre:	11.10.11.10.

3.6 I Sing the Birth (p. 109)

Date of composition:	1928 (completed on 30 October)
Setting:	SATB unaccompanied
Manuscript sources:	A) Rough score: BL Add MS 58965
	B) Vocal score: Birthplace MS 43
First published:	Novello, 1928
First performance:	10 December 1928, Royal Albert Hall, London
Key:	A minor, but with modal implications
Tempo:	Allegretto
Number of bars:	72
Text author:	Ben Jonson (1572-1637) Alleluias added

3.7 Good Morrow (p. 109)

Date of composition:	1929

APPENDIX ONE

Setting:	SATB unaccompanied
Manuscript sources:	A) Sketches: Birthplace MS 32
	B) Score: BL Add MS 58066
First published:	Novello, 1929
Current edition:	Novello
First performance:	9 December 1929, St George's Chapel, Windsor Castle
Key:	B flat major
Tempo:	Allegretto
Number of bars:	80
Text author:	George Gascoigne (?1525-1577)

Appendix Two

Specification of the organ at St George's Catholic Church, Worcester, as it was during Elgar's period as organist there:

Great Organ

		Swell Organ	
Open Diapason	8'	Open Diapason	8'
Keraulaphone	8'	Lieblich Gedeckt	8'
Dulciana	8'	Voix Celeste	8'
Clarabella	8'	Salicional	8'
Principal	4'	Flute	4'
Harmonic Flute	4'	Piccolo	2'
		Oboe	8'

Pedal Organ

		Couplers
Large Bourdon	16'	Swell to Great
Small Bourdon	16'	Swell to Pedal
		Great to Pedal

Note: Correspondence and papers relating to the condition of the organ, and subsequent rebuilding, are preserved at the Jesuit Archives, Farm Street Church, London.

Bibliography

Andrews, Hilda. *Westminster Retrospect: A memoir of Sir Richard Terry*. Oxford University Press. 1948.
Anderson, Robert. *Elgar*. J.M. Dent. 1993.
Anonymous. 'New Choral Setting of Psalm XLVIII, by Edward Elgar'. *The Musical Times* 53: 584-585. 1912.
Atkins, E. Wulstan. *The Elgar Atkins Friendship*. David and Charles. 1984.
Bax, Arnold. *Farewell, My Youth*. Longmans, Green and Co. 1943.
Buckley, Robert J. *Sir Edward Elgar*. 2nd edition. John Lane: The Bodley Head. 1912.
Burley, Rosa, and Carruthers, Frank. *Edward Elgar: the Record of a Friendship*. Barrie and Jenkins. 1972.
Butcher, Vernon. *The Organs and Music of Worcester Cathedral*. 1981.
de Cordova, Rudolph. 'Dr Edward Elgar'. *The Strand Magazine*. May 1904: 537-544.
De-la-Noy, Michael. *Elgar: The Man*. Hamish Hamilton. 1988.
Dennison, Peter. 'Elgar and Wagner'. *Music & Letters* 66(2): 93-109. 1985.
Dunhill, Thomas. *Sir Edward Elgar*. Blackie & Son. 1938.
Edwards, F.G. 'Edward Elgar'. *The Musical Times* (1 October 1900) 41: 641-648.
Elgar, Edward. *A Future for English Music and Other Lectures by Edward Elgar*. Edited by Percy M. Young. Dennis Dobson. 1968.
Fenby, Eric. *Delius As I Knew Him*. Bell. 1936.
Gaisberg, F.W. *Music on Record*. Robert Hale. 1946.
Goosens, Eugene. *Overture and Beginners*. Methuen & Co. London. 1951.

Hamilton, G.H. *The Art and Architecture of Russia*. Harmondsworth. 1954.

Hodgkins, Geoffrey. *Providence and Art: A study in Elgar's religious beliefs*. Elgar Society. 1979.

Houfe, Simon. *Sir Albert Richardson: The Professor*. White Crescent Press. 1980.

Howes, Frank. *The English Musical Renaissance*. Secker & Warburg. 1966.

Hurd, Michael. *Vincent Novello — and Company*. Granada Publishing. 1981.

Kennedy, Michael. *Portrait of Elgar*. 3rd edition. Oxford University Press. 1987.

Lightwood, J.T. *Samuel Wesley*. 1937.

Maine, Basil. *Elgar: His Life and Works*. Vols I & II. G. Bell & Sons. 1933.

Massey, Bernard S. 'The Hymn Tunes of Elgar and Holst'. *Bulletin of The Hymn Society of Great Britain and Ireland* 10 (8): 185-188. 1984.

McVeagh, Diana M. *Edward Elgar: His Life and Music*. J.M. Dent & Sons. 1955.

Moore, Jerrold Northrop. *Elgar on Record*. Oxford University Press. 1974.

———. *Edward Elgar: A Creative Life*. Oxford University Press. 1984a.

———. *Spirit of England: Elgar in his World*. Heinemann. 1984b.

———. *Elgar and His Publishers: Letters of a Creative Life*. Vols I & II. Oxford University Press. 1987.

———. *Edward Elgar: The Windflower Letters*. Oxford University Press. 1989.

———. *Edward Elgar: Letters of a Lifetime*. Oxford University Press. 1990.

Nettel, R. *Music in the Five Towns: 1840 - 1914*. Oxford University Press. 1944.

Parrot, Ian. *Elgar*. J.M. Dent & Sons. 1971.

Pearson, Hesketh. *Bernard Shaw: His Life and Personality*. Collins. 1942.

Reed, W.H.. *Elgar*. J.M Dent & Sons. 1939.

———. *Elgar as I Knew Him*. Victor Gollancz. 1973.

Scholes, Percy. 'Sir Edward Elgar at Home'. *The Music Student* 8(2):

343-348. 1916.

Talbot, G. Surtees. 'Elgar as a Writer of Church Anthems'. *The Music Student* 8(2): 364. 1916.

Trahair, Christine Anne. 'The Early Church Music of Edward Elgar'. Unpublished M.A. thesis. University of Melbourne. 1983.

Willetts, Pamela. 'The Elgar sketchbooks'. *The British Library Journal* 11(1): 25-45. 1985.

Young, Percy M. *Elgar O.M.: A Study of a Musician*. Collins. 1955.

———(ed.). *Letters of Edward Elgar and other writings*. Geoffrey Bles. 1956.

———(ed.). *Letters to Nimrod: Edward Elgar to August Jaeger, 1897 - 1908*. Dennis Dobson. 1965.

———. *A History of British Music*. Ernest Benn. 1967.

———. *Alice Elgar: Enigma of a Victorian Lady*. Dennis Dobson. 1978.

———. 'Edward Elgar — Music for the Catholic Liturgy'. *American Choral Review* 28(1): 3-10. 1986.

Acknowledgements

It is a pleasure to recall the names of the many people without whose help this book could not have been written. Much of the original research was done for a thesis I submitted to the University of Cape Town in 1989, so I renew my thanks to those who assisted me then: Michael Kennedy, Donald Hunt, E. Wulstan Atkins, Robert Anderson, Christopher Kent, Christopher Barends, Ursula Brett, Bernard S. Massey, Geoffrey Hodgkins, and Fr J. Duggan, SJ (formerly of St George's Catholic Church, Worcester).

I have received help from James and Christopher Bennett of the Birthplace Museum, Broadheath, and from many librarians. In particular, I acknowledge the assistance of Fr T.G. Holt, SJ, the archivist of the Jesuit Archives, Farm Street Church, London, the staff of the Manuscripts Department of the British Library, the staff of the W.H. Bell Music Library and Jagger Library, University of Cape Town, the Hereford and Worcester County Record Office, and the Baillieu Library at the University of Melbourne.

Two people gave guidance and encouragement to both thesis and book: my original university supervisor Barry Smith, and Jerrold Northrop Moore, who generously shared his knowledge. Both Andrew Porter and Diana McVeagh kindly read this book and offered invaluable criticism. I must acknowledge the help of John Powell Ward, who commissioned the book. Finally, I owe a special debt to the moral support of my wife Nicole.

Series Afterword

The Border country is that region between England and Wales which is upland and lowland, both and neither. Centuries ago kings and barons fought over these Marches without their national allegience ever being settled. In our own time, referring to his childhood, that eminent borderman Raymond Williams once said: 'We talked of "The English" who were not us, and "The Welsh" who were not us'. It is beautiful, gentle, intriuging and often surprising. It displays majestic landscapes, which show a lot, and hide some more. People now walk it, poke into its cathedrals and bookshops, and fly over or hang-glide from its mountains, yet its mystery remains.

In cultural terms the region is as fertile as (in parts) its agriculture and soil. The continued success of the Three Choirs Festival and the growth of the border town of Hay as a centre of the secondhand book trade have both attracted international recognition. The present series of introductory books is offered in the light of such events. Writers as diverse as Mary Webb, Raymond Williams and Wilfred Owen are seen in the special light — perhaps that cloudy, golden twilight so characteristic of the region — of their origin in this area or association with it. There are titles too, though fewer, on musicians and painters. The Gloucestershire composers such as Samuel Sebastian Wesley, and painters like David Jones, bear an imprint of border woods, rivers, villages and hills.

How wide is the border? Two, five or fifteen miles each side of the boundary; it depends on your perspective, on the placing of the nearest towns, on the terrain itself, and on history. In the time of Offa and after, Hereford itself was a frontier town, and Welsh was spoken there even in the nineteenth century. True border folk traditionally did not recognize those from even a few miles away. Today, with greater mobility, the crossing of boundaries is easier, whether for education, marriage, art or leisure. For myself, who spent some childhood years in Herefordshire and a decade of middle-age crossing between England and Wales once a week, I can only say that as you approach the border you feel it. Suddenly you are in that finally elusive terrain, looking from a bare height down onto the plain, or from the lower land up to a gap in the hills, and you want to explore it, maybe not to return.

This elusiveness pertains to the writers and artisits too. It is often difficult to decide who is border, to what extent and with what impact on their work. The urbane Elizabeth Barrett Browning, prominent figure of the salons of London and Italy in her time, spent virtually all her life until her late twenties outside Ledbury in Herefordshire, and this fact is being seen by current critics and scholars as of more and more significance. The twentieth century 'English pastoral' composers — with names like Parry, Howells, and Vaughan Williams — were nearly all border people. One wonders whether border country is now suddenly found on the English side of the Severn Bridge, and how far even John Milton's *Comus*, famous for its first production in Ludlow Castle, is in any sense such a work. Then there is the fascinating Uxbridge-born Peggy Eileen Whistler, transposed in the 1930s into Margiad Evans to write her (epilepsis-based) visionary novels set near her adored Ross-on-Wye and which today still retain a magical charm. Further north: could Barbara Pym, born and raised in Oswestry, even remotely be called a border writer? Most people would say that the poet A.E. Housman was far more so, yet he hardly ever visited the county after which his chief book of poems, *A Shropshire Lad*, is named. Further north still: there is the village of Chirk on the boundary itself, where R.S. Thomas had his first curacy; there is Gladstone's Hawardan Library, just outside Chester and actually into Clwyd in Wales itself; there is intruigingly the Wirral town of Birkenhead, where Wilfred Owen spent his adolescence and where his fellow war poet Hedd Wyn was awarded his Chair — posthumously.

On the Welsh side the names are different. The mystic Ann Griffiths; the metaphysical poet Henry Vaughan; the astonishing nineteenth century symbolist novelist Arthur Machen (in Linda

Dowling's phrase, 'Pater's prose as registered by Wilde'); and the remarkable Thomas Olivers of Gregynog, associated with the writing of the well-known hymn 'Lo He comes with clouds descending'. Those descending clouds...; in border country the scene hangs overhead, and it is easy to indulge in unwarranted speculation. Most significant perhaps is the difference to the two peoples on either side. From England, the border meant the enticement of emptiness, a strange unpopulated land, going up and up into the hills. From Wales, the border meant the road to London, to the university, or to employment, whether by droving sheep, or later to the industries of Birmingham and Liverpool. It also meant the enemy, since borders and boundaries are necessarily political. Much is shared, yet different languages are spoken, in more than one sense.

With certain notable exceptions, the books in this series are short introductory studies of one person's work or some aspect of it. There are no indexes. The bibliography lists main sources referred to in the text and sometimes others, for anyone who would like to pursue the topic further. The authors reflect the diversity of their subjects. They are specialists or academics; critics or biographers; poets or musicians themselves; or ordinary people with, however, an established reputation of writing imaginatively and directly about what moves them. They are of various ages, both sexes, Welsh and English, border people themselves or from further afield.

To those who explore the matter, the subjects — the writers, painters and composers written about — seem increasingly united by a particular kind of vision. This holds good however diverse they are in other, main ways; and of course they are diverse indeed. One might scarcely associate, it would seem, Raymond Williams with Samuel Sebastian Wesley, or Dennis Potter with Thomas Traherne. But one has to be careful in such assumptions. The epigraph to Bruce Chatwin's twentieth century novel *On the Black Hill* is a passage from the seventeeth century mystic writer Jeremy Taylor. Thomas Traherne himself is the subject of a recent American study which puts Traherne's writings into dialogue with the European philosopher-critics Martin Heidegger, Jacques Derrida and Jacques Lacan. And a current bestselling writer of thrillers, Ellis Peters, sets her stories in a Shrewsbury of the late medieval Church with a cunning quiet monk as her ever-engaging sleuth.

The vision (name incidentally of the farmhouse in Chatwin's novel) is something to do with the curious border light already mentioned. To avoid getting sentimental and mystic here — though border writers have at times been both — one might suggest literally that this effect is meteorological. Maybe the sun's rays are refracted through skeins of dew or mist that hit the stark mountains and low hills at curious ascertainable angles, with prismatic results. Not that rainbows are the point in our area: it is more the contrasts of gold, green and grey. Some writers never mention it. They don't have to. But all the artists of the region see it, are affected by it, and transpose their highly different emanations of reality through its transparencies. Meanwhile, on the ground, the tourist attractions draw squads from diverse cultural and ethnic origins; agriculture enters the genetic-engineering age; New Age travellers are welcome and unwelcome; and the motorway runs up paralled past all — 'Lord of the M5', as the poet Geoffrey Hill has dubbed the Saxon king Offa, he of the dyke which bisects the region where it can still be identified. The region has it uniqueness, then, and a statistically above-average number of writers and artists (we have identified over fifty clear candidates so far) have drawn something from it, which it is the business of this present series to elucidate.

Edward Elgar, most English of composers in the eyes (ears) of most partly-thinking English persons, moved to Hereford in 1904 and at once referred to 'that sweet borderland which I have made my home'. He was hardly a true borderman of the England-Wales strip as that is usually conceived, being of Worcestershire, which is not even a neighbouring county. Yet that terrain affected him all his life, possibly because it spoke to the boundary condition he knew too painfully in religious, social and musical dimensions. John Allison has told the story as it relates to the church music (and so Elgar's ambivalent position as a Catholic), and no addition is needed here. This specialist narrative has not been previously attempted in this fashion, nor the music and the life so immaculately interwoven.